Samuel Hopkins

An Inquiry Concerning the Future State of Those Who Die in Their

Sins

Wherein the dictates of Scripture and reason upon this important subject are

carefully considered, and whether endless punishment be consistent with divine

justice, wisdom and goodness

Samuel Hopkins

An Inquiry Concerning the Future State of Those Who Die in Their Sins
Wherein the dictates of Scripture and reason upon this important subject are carefully considered, and whether endless punishment be consistent with divine justice, wisdom and goodness

ISBN/EAN: 9783337425913

Printed in Europe, USA, Canada, Australia, Japan

Cover: Foto ©Lupo / pixelio.de

More available books at www.hansebooks.com

AN

INQUIRY

CONCERNING

The future State of those who die in their Sins;

Wherein the DICTATES of SCRIPTURE And REASON, on this important SUBJECT, Are carefully considered;

And whether ENDLESS PUNISHMENT be CONSISTENT With Divine JUSTICE, WISDOM and GOODNESS: In which also OBJECTIONS are stated and answered.

By *SAMUEL HOPKINS*, A. M.
Pastor of the first Congregational Church in NEWPORT.

O, that they were wise, that they understood this,
THAT THEY WOULD CONSIDER THEIR LATTER END!
JEHOVAH.

NEWPORT, *Rhode-Island*:
Printed by *SOLOMON SOUTHWICK*, 1783.

ADVERTISEMENT.

THE Substance of the following Inquiry was written some Years ago, soon after the Doctrine of endless Punishment began to be publicly denied by some among us. Last Winter it was revised; and some Additions and Alterations were made; by which it has been cast into the Form in which it now appears.

Since it was finished, the Author has seen several late Publications on the same Subject; in which are found some of the same Sentiments and Arguments, which are introduced by him.* But, as they were not taken from them, and are not expressed in the same Manner, or introduced in the same Connexion here; and as this Attempt is designed to be a more particular and full Discussion of the Subject; and may fall into the Hands of some, who will not see those mentioned; it is hoped this Publication, after them, will not be thought assuming or needless.

* The Doctrine of final, Universal Salvation examined and shewn to be unscriptural. By Dr. Gordon, of Roxbury.—A Discourse concerning the Process of the General Judgment. By Mr. Emmons, of Franklin.—That all Men shall not be saved, attempted to be proved and illustrated, in three Sermons. By Mr. Thacker, of Malden.

Newport, May 6, 1783.

Introduction. Page i―――vi.

SECTION I. In which it is inquired, whether the Wicked will be punished in the future State; and what the Holy Scriptures teach concerning this. Page 1―――53.

SECTION II. Wherein it is particularly considered, whether it is revealed in the Holy Scriptures, that the Punishment of the Wicked will be *endless*. Page 54―――85.

SECTION III. Containing an Examination of those Passages of Scripture, which the Opposers of the Doctrine of endless Punishment, and Advocates for the Salvation of all Men, have thought to be favorable to their Cause.
Page 85―――118.

SECTION IV. Wherein it is considered, what *Reason* may be given for the Doctrine of endless Punishment, which is revealed in the Scriptures; or *why* God will punish impenitent Sinners forever: And whether there be any reasonable Objections against this.
Page 119―――155.

SECTION V. Containing a Number of Questions and Answers, relating to the Doctrine of endless Punishment. Page 156―――175.

SECTION VI. Containing Inferences from the Doctrine of endless Punishment; and a particular Improvement of it. Page 176―194.

THE INTRODUCTION.

MAN is not only made capable of looking forward, but is strongly inclined to do it, and cannot avoid a greater or less degree of thought and concern about futurity, and the good or evil which he shall be the subject of *hereafter.* These are the objects of all his hopes and fears, and afford great scope for the continual exercise of them, and those affections which attend them; by which he is influenced, more or less, in all his conduct. And though most of mankind appear to confine their prospects chiefly or altogether within the narrow limits of this life, and feel little concerned about that which may take place after they leave this world; yet who is there that will not pronounce this very unreasonable, on the least serious reflection, and consider it as an evidence, among a thousand others, of human depravity?

We are certainly capable of existence in a future state; yea, of continuing to exist without end; and there is nothing in reason or experience to render this improbable; but much to induce us to believe, that this present life is only preparatory to our existing in an endless state hereafter; and that we shall be happy or miserable there, according as we are the objects of the favor of our Maker, or not. Therefore, this our future existence is the most interesting and important to us, and demands our greatest and most serious attention, and concern, and the highest exercise of our hopes and fears.

It is true, indeed, that when we turn our thoughts to this subject, we at once feel that reason alone will never enable us to determine, without hesitation, many important inquiries about a future state; and that mankind would be left in great and most undesirable uncertainty and darkness, respecting all things that relate to the invisible world, without some other assistance; and that it is therefore greatly desirable, and of infinite importance, that God, who is able, should assist man, by a particular revelation of his will and design, with regard to a future state. And this might not only be a ground of hope that God may thus favor his creature man, to whom he grants so many favors in his providence, and shows himself propitious; but affords good reason to conclude he has actually given such a revelation: And may serve to excite *our* gratitude to God, who find ourselves in actual possession of a revelation which bears every mark, and is attended with all the evidence of its divine original, that can be desired, or even conceived; and ought to lead us to feel the great obligations we are under to attend to it, with a serious and honest mind, ready to receive the dictates of heaven, on this important point, whatever we may find to be revealed. All

All who admit the scriptures of the old and new-testaments to be from God, agree that it is there revealed, that they who shall be redeemed from sin, and made happy by Christ the Saviour, shall have an unceasing existence in perfect happiness in his everlasting kingdom. But they have differed much about the future existence and punishment of those who do not embrace the gospel in this life; but live and die in their sins. Most who have lived in the christian world have professed to believe, that it is as clearly revealed that the latter shall exist forever in endless punishment, as that the former shall be happy without end. But a number have denied this. Some have expressed a confidence that all the wicked shall cease to exist, and be annihilated, either immediately upon the death of the body, or after they have continued in misery, and been punished during a proper length of time. Others are confident, it can be proved from scripture, that all the human race will be finally and eternally happy. Some of these allow, that they who die in their sins will be punished for a season, even after the day of judgment, as an effectual discipline to bring them to repentance. But others confidently assert that all will be happy at the day of judgment. And some of these hold that all do enter into perfect blessedness, when they leave this world.

The design of the following inquiry is to assist

sist all who are desirous to know the truth, in examining this point in the light of the sacred oracles; and to help them to see the reasonableness of what is there revealed concerning it, and to answer the most material objections that have been made against it. There seems to be a special call for this *now*, as the denial of endless punishment has been more open and common of late, and the doctrine of universal salvation, though in different forms, is zealously espoused by many.

We have no reason to think the difference of sentiment on so important and interesting a point, among those who profess to form their different opinions from divine revelation, is owing to any defect in the bible, or because the truth respecting it is not revealed with sufficient plainness. This diversity and opposition of sentiment, therefore, must be wholly owing to the faulty prejudices, and evil biases in the minds of men, which indispose them to believe the truth, and lead them to misunderstand and pervert the holy scriptures; even where that which is revealed is very plain and decisive.

Whoever attends to the different and opposite sentiments on almost every point in religion, which have been and are embraced, even by those who have the bible in their hands, and appeal to that for the support of what they believe, will have sufficient reason to determine, that no standing revelation can be given from

heaven

heaven, however perfect, plain and decisive, that cannot be misunderstood and perverted, by men of corrupt and perverse minds. If divine revelation be so formed, that they cannot fail of seeing every important truth contained in it, who give suitable attention to it, and have a meek, humble, honest mind; it is suited to answer all the desirable ends of a revelation, however it may be abused and perverted, by those who do not love the truth, in support of the most gross and hurtful errors.

We therefore have all desirable encouragement to search the scriptures, that we may learn what will be the certain consequence of living and dying in sin; what will be the punishment of the wicked in the future state; as it is certainly there plainly revealed; and however men have differed, and many have run into great and dangerous errors on this point, we may have the comfortable assurance, that we shall know what is the truth respecting this important article, if with meekness and impartiality we be ready to receive and love what God has revealed. But as many have failed of this, and have come to the bible full of prejudices against the truth there revealed, and disposed to believe nothing contained in divine revelation, which is not agreeable to their corrupted minds; and so have not believed the truth, and have been justly given up to strong delusion, to believe a lie; and we are liable to the same sin,

and

and dreadful consequence; let us therefore take heed to ourselves, and humbly, with earnestness and constancy, look to the Father of lights, that he may give us an honest heart, and so open our minds to understand the scriptures, that we may find the truth after which we are now inquiring, and have our hearts established in it, and be directed to improve it to his glory, our own eternal good, and the benefit of our neighbour.

SECTION I.

SECTION I.

IN which it is inquired, whether the Wicked will be punished in the future State; and what the holy Scriptures teach concerning this.

MUCH is said in the scripture concerning the evil and punishment that will come on the wicked in a future state. This observation will be sufficiently illustrated by the following passages; though they do not contain all that is said on this subject in the inspired writings.

The evils which God brings on men in this world for their sins, and his often destroying them in a terrible manner, as a testimony of his displeasure with them, many instances of which we find recorded in sacred writ, do forebode the future punishment of the wicked, and may well be considered as a standing evidence and admonition of this. * The

---

* It is true indeed, that many make the evils they suffer in this life, an argument that they shall be happy in the future world, and are hence confident, as it has been often expressed, that all the hell they shall have, is in this world.

But

The destruction of the old world by the flood, when only one family was saved; the overthrow of Sodom and Gomorrah, and the deliverance of Lot, are considered, by Christ and his apostles, as emblems or types of the destruction or punishment of the wicked in the future state, and the salvation of God's people. Mat. xxvi. 37, 38. "But as the days of Noah were, so shall also the coming of the Son of man be. For as in the days that were before the flood, they were eating and drinking, &c. until the day that Noah entered into the ark, and knew not till the flood came and took them all away; *so shall also the coming of the Son of man be.*" 2 Pet. ii. 5, &c. "For if God spared not the old world, but saved Noah, bringing in the flood upon the world of the ungodly; and turning the cities of Sodom and Gomorrah into ashes, condemned them with an overthrow, *making them an ensample to those that after should live ungodly*; and delivered just Lot. The Lord knoweth how to deliver the godly out of temptation, *and to reserve the unjust unto the day of judgment to be punished.*" Here the apostle makes these destructions of the wicked an argument that the ungodly in general will be punished in the future

But this way of arguing is evidently owing to their being insensible and greatly stupid, with respect to the evil of sin, and the magnitude of their own crimes, and their looking on themselves in a measure innocent. Hence they conclude, that the evils they suffer here in body and mind, are full as much as they deserve, and indeed *a great deal more.*

ture ſtate, and after the day of judgment: And therefore teaches us to conſider them in this light, and by them to learn the diſtinction God will make between the godly and unjuſt at the laſt day. In the ſame light St. Jude conſiders the deſtruction of Sodom, &c. "Even as Sodom and Gomorrah, giving themſelves over to fornication, and going after ſtrange fleſh, *are ſet forth for an example ſuffering the vengeance of eternal fire.*" In this way, the bible is full of admonitions of the ſure puniſhment of all that live ungodly, when the righteous ſhall be completely delivered, and enter into everlaſting life. A contrary doom is pointed out for the wicked.

When God reveals a Saviour, by Moſes, and promiſeth he ſhall come into the world, in the character of a prophet, he adds the following words, Deut xviii. 19. "And it ſhall come to paſs that whoſoever will not hearken unto my words, which he ſhall ſpeak in my name, *I will require it of him.*" That is, he ſhall anſwer to me for it, and I will deal with him, and puniſh him accordingly. Therefore when St. Peter quotes this paſſage, he expreſſes the true ſenſe in the following words, "He ſhall be deſtroyed from among his people." This is an early declaration, that rejection of Chriſt in this world, would prove fatal to men; and that he would be ſo far from *ſaving all men*, that they who ſhall diſregard him in this life, will certainly be

C   puniſhed

punished with a peculiarly aggravated destruction.

We find an awful threatning of God to the wicked, who continue his incorrigible enemies, through this life, under all the methods taken to reclaim them, in Deut. xxxii. 35, &c. "To me belongeth vengeance and recompence, their foot shall slide in due time; for the day of their calamity is at hand, and the things that shall come upon them make haste. For I lift my hand to heaven, and say I live forever. If I whet my glittering sword, and mine hand take hold on judgment; I will render vengeance to mine enemies, and will reward them that hate me. I will make mine arrows drunk with blood, and that with the blood of the slain, and of the captives, from the beginning of revenges upon the enemy."

The punishment here threatened, to the obstinately wicked, is to be inflicted in a future state; for no such distinction between God's people and his enemies, as is represented in this passage of scripture, does take place in this world: Besides, the first words of this paragraph are quoted by St. Paul, Heb. x. 30, and he applies them to the future punishment of the wicked, of which he is there speaking. "For we know him that hath said, Vengeance belongeth unto me, I will recompense, saith the Lord." And he then adds, "It is a fearful thing to fall into the hands of the living God." In the last words,

The

The living God, he evidently has reference to those in the paſſage above recited, " I lift my hand to heaven, and ſay, *I live forever.*" Which certainly implies, that God lives ſo as to be able to puniſh the wicked in a future ſtate; ſo that they are ſo far from getting out of his hands when they die, that then in a peculiar ſenſe, they *fall into his hands*, to ſuffer the vengeance threatened. And may it not be juſtly obſerved here, that, though the endleſs duration of this puniſhment is not expreſly aſſerted in the threatning; yet it ſeems to be plainly intimated, when Jehovah introduces himſelf as *living forever*, to expreſs his determination and ability to render vengeance and recompence to his enemies; and that he will do this as long as he liveth. But this is to be more particularly conſidered hereafter. And perhaps it will appear, when properly conſidered, that it is neceſſary that God ſhould live forever in order to render vengeance, and a proper and full recompence to his enemies, that is, a puniſhment equal to their deſert.

Job and his friends ſpeak much of the evil end, and puniſhment of the wicked, as certain and inevitable; being the objects of God's diſpleaſure and wrath; and at the ſame time mention the ſecurity and happineſs of the righteous, in his favor and protection. See Job iv. 8, 9, 20, 21. viii. 13,—22. xi. 13.—20. xv. 20, —35. xviii. 5,—21. xx. 4,—29. In this laſt quoted

quoted passage are the following words, "Knowest thou not this of old, that the triumphing of the wicked is short, and the joy of the hypocrite but for a moment? Though his excellency mount up to the heavens, and his head reach unto the clouds; yet he shall perish forever, like his own dung—His bones are full of the sins of his youth; which shall lie down with him in the dust. When he is about to fill his belly, God shall cast the fury of his wrath upon him, and shall rain it upon him while he is eating. He shall flee from the iron weapon, and a bow of steel shall strike him through. It is drawn and cometh out of the body; yea the glistering sword cometh out of his gall; terrors are upon him. A fire not blown shall consume him. The heaven shall reveal his iniquity; and the earth shall rise up against him. This is the portion of *a wicked man* from God, and the heritage appointed unto him by God." Job himself agrees with his friends in this, that the wicked are the objects of God's wrath, and shall be punished. They differed on this head only in *applying* this doctrine: *They* considered outward afflictions in this world, as included in the punishment of the wicked; and therefore concluded, that they who suffered greatly by the hand of God in this life, were ungodly, and the objects of divine displeasure; and that God would protect and save the truly pious from such evils, in this world. *He* insisted, that the distinction between the

righteous

righteous and the wicked did not take place, and appear in God's difpenfations and dealings with them, in his providence, in this life; therefore the good and evil by which they were to be diftinguifhed, muft and would take place in a future ftate only. He fays, that innocence and righteoufnefs will not fecure a perfon from afflictions in this life, and from death, in common with the wicked. Chap ix. 22, &c. " This is one thing, therefore I faid it, he deftroyeth the perfect and the wicked. If the fcourge flay fuddenly, he will laugh at the trial of the innocent. The earth is given into the hands of the wicked; if not, where, and who is he?" He obferves, that the wicked live long and profper in their wickednefs in this world, Chap. xii. 6. " The tabernacles of robbers profper, and they that provoke God are fecure, into whofe hand God bringeth abundantly." Chap. xxi. 7, 8, 9. " Wherefore do the wicked live, become old, yea, and mighty in power? Their feed is eftablifhed in their fight with them, and their offspring before their eyes. Their houfes are fafe from fear, neither is the rod of God upon them, &c." Yet he fpeaks of the punifhment and deftruction of the wicked as certain and inevitable; which therefore muft take place in a future ftate. Speaking of the wicked, he fays, " They are as ftubble before the wind, and as chaff that the ftorm carrieth away. God layeth up his iniquity for his children: He rewardeth him,

him, and he shall know it. His eyes shall see his destruction, and he shall drink of the wrath of the Almighty." Chap. xxvii. 7, &c. "Let mine enemy be as the wicked, and he that riseth up against me, as the unrighteous. For what is the hope of the hypocrite, though he hath gained, when God taketh away his soul? Will God hear his cry when trouble cometh upon him? This is the portion of the wicked man with God, and the heritage of oppressors, which they shall receive of the Almighty. The rich man shall lie down, but he shall not be gathered." i. e. he shall die, but shall not be gathered and received to the society of the blessed, as Abraham, Isaac and Jacob were at their death. "He openeth his eyes, and he is not. Terrors take hold on him as waters, a tempest stealeth him away in the night. The east wind carrieth him away, and he departeth; and a storm hurleth him out of his place. For God shall cast upon him, and not spare: He would fain flee out of his hand." Chap. xxxi. 3. "Is not destruction to the wicked, and a strange punishment to the workers of iniquity?"

Job and his friends lived in the days of Moses, or before; and by them we learn what was the doctrine respecting the future punishment of the wicked, received and taught by the people of God at that time. They represent it as certain and very dreadful, and give not the least hint, that it shall ever end; but the whole they say,
rather

rather imports the contrary. They reprefent the wicked as deprived of all his hopes, when he dies; which furely can not be true, if he fhall be immediately happy, or happy forever, though punifhed for a time. *What is the hope of the hypocrite, though he hath gained, when God taketh away his foul ? God fhall caft upon him,* AND NOT SPARE. Yea, *he fhall perifh forever.*

The book of Pfalms, in which the future ftate is brought more fully into view, than in the preceding part of fcripture, is full of threatnings to finners, and declarations of their punifhment in the world to come. This will be fufficiently evident, by reciting the following paffages, out of many more which are found in thofe facred writings.

In the firft Pfalm the truly pious are pronounced bleffed; and the ungodly are curfed, as thofe who fhall be condemned at the day of judgment, feparated from the righteous, and utterly perifh, and be deftroyed. " The ungodly are not fo: but are like the chaff which the wind driveth away. Therefore the ungodly fhall not ftand in the judgment, nor finners in the congregation of the righteous : For the Lord knoweth the way of the righteous; but the way of the ungodly fhall perifh." Pfal. xi. 6. Upon the wicked he fhall rain fnares, fire and brimftone, and an horrible tempeft : This fhall be the portion of their cup." This is not their portion in this life ; therefore it muft refer to their punifhment nishment in a future state; which is represented as very dreadful. Psal. xxi. 8, 9. "Thine hand shall find out all thine enemies, thy right hand shall find out those that hate thee. Thou shalt make them as a fiery oven in the time of thine anger: The Lord shall swallow them up, and the fire shall devour them." xxxiv. 21. "Evil shall slay the wicked; and they that hate the righteous shall be desolate." When the Psalmist has related the trouble and perplexity he had experienced, by observing the apparent prosperity and happiness of the wicked in this world, he says, Psal. lxxiii. 17, &c. "When I thought to know this, it was too painful for me; until I went into the sanctuary of God; then understood I their *end*. Surely thou didst set them in slippery places: Thou castedest them down into destruction. How are they brought into desolation as in a moment! They are utterly consumed with terrors. As a dream when one awaketh; so, O Lord, when thou awakest, thou shalt despise their image. For lo, they that are far from thee shall perish: Thou hast destroyed all them that go a whoring from thee." All this evil, wretchedness and destruction, in which the wicked perish, is what must be inflicted on them after death, in the invisible world; for these are they who prosper in this world, and die like other men, as death is common to both the righteous and wicked. Their *end* therefore, which he then understood and described, must

be

be the punishment which comes on the wicked in consequence of death, or leaving this world. If the wicked were happy as soon as they leave this world, this passage would be altogether unintelligible; yea, a perfect deception. And how can there be any end to this destruction and punishment, when this itself is said to be their *end?* If this destruction were to come to an end, and they, after all, must be eternally happy, how can this be called *their end?* When St. Paul speaks of some whose *end* is destruction, must he not intend a destruction which is inconsistent with their eternal happiness? For if he meant a destruction consistent with their having eternal life, such a destruction is not *their end*, but infinitely far from it; and everlasting life would be *their end*: And there would be no propriety or truth in the distinction which he makes. Rom. vi. 21, 22. " What fruit had ye then in those things, whereof ye are now ashamed? For *the end of those things is death.* But now being made free from sin, and become servants to God, ye have your fruit unto holiness, *and the end everlasting life.*"

Psal. lxxv. 8. " In the hand of the Lord there is a cup, and the wine is red: It is full of mixture, and he poureth out the same; but the dregs thereof all the wicked of the earth shall wring them out, and drink them." xcii. 7, 8, 9. When the wicked spring as the grass, and when all the workers of iniquity do flourish, it is that they shall be destroyed forever. But thou, Lord, art most high forevermore For lo, thine enemies, O Lord, for lo, thine enemies shall perish." xciv. 23. "And he shall bring upon them their own iniquity; and shall cut them off in their own wickedness; yea, the Lord our God shall cut them off." cxii. 9, 10. "His righteousness (who feareth the Lord) endureth forever; his horn shall be exalted with honour. The wicked shall see it, and be grieved; he shall gnash with his teeth, and melt away: The desire of the wicked shall perish." This distinction between the righteous and the wicked is not made in this life; therefore it must be made in the future state; and then this threatning shall be inflicted on the wicked. cxxxix. 19. "Surely, thou wilt slay the wicked, O God." This does not intend God's taking them out of the world by death; for in this sense, he slays the righteous as much as the wicked; but it must intend a punishment after the death of the body, or the second death, or it can have no meaning. This is evidently opposed to what David desires God would grant unto him, ver. 24, "Lead me in the *way everlasting.*" cxlv. 20. "The Lord preserveth all them that love him; but all the wicked will he destroy." This also must refer to a future state; for both they who love God, and his enemies, are equally preserved in this life, and destroyed by dying. This destruction of the wicked is

that

that which is so often spoken of as their portion and end, in the future state.

In the writings of Solomon, especially in his Proverbs, we find the future punishment and misery of the wicked often mentioned; and generally in contrast to the safety and happiness of the righteous. The following instances, out of many more that might be mentioned, will be sufficient to illustrate this remark. Prov. i. 24, &c. "Because I have called, and ye refused, I have stretched out my hand, and no man regarded; but ye have set at nought my counsel, and would none of my reproof: I also will laugh at your calamity, and I will mock when your fear cometh; when your fear cometh as desolation, and your destruction cometh as a whirlwind; when distress and anguish cometh upon you. Then shall they call upon me, but I will not answer; they shall seek me early, but shall not find me. For that they hated knowledge, and did not chuse the fear of the Lord: Therefore shall they eat of the fruit of their own way, and be filled with their own devices. For the turning away of the simple shall slay them, and the prosperity of fools shall destroy them." Chap. v. 22, "His own iniquities shall take the wicked himself, and he shall be holden with the cords of his sins. He shall die without instruction, and in the greatness of his folly he shall go astray." Chap. x. 28. "The hope of the righteous shall be gladness: But the expectation of the wicked shall perish. The way of the Lord is strength to the upright: But destruction to the workers of iniquity." Chap. xi. 7. When a wicked man dieth his expectation shall perish: And the hope of unjust men perisheth." What words could more fully express the misery of the wicked after death, or assert more strongly, that he shall then be deprived of all good, which is the object of hope, and fall into absolute despair? And how inconsistent are such assertions as these, with his surviving this misery, and, after all this, obtaining eternal happiness! How can his hope perish when he dies, if he knows, or has the least hope, that he shall be yet eternally happy? Chap. xxiii. 17, 18. Solomon says, "Let not thine heart envy sinners: But be thou in the fear of the Lord all the day long: For surely there is an end, and thy expectation shall not be cut off." These words illustrate those last quoted. If this be a promise to him that feareth God, that he shall be happy after death, and that without end, as it certainly is; then the other is a threatning of the contrary, which is misery without end. If both the righteous and the wicked shall be happy together, forever; how is it possible to be true, that the hope of the latter shall be cut off and perish, when he dies; and directly the contrary be true of the former?

Chap. xi. 21. "Though hand join in hand, the wicked shall not be unpunished." Chap. xii.

xii. 7. "The wicked are overthrown and are not; but the house of the righteous shall stand." Chap. xiii. 21. "Evil pursueth sinners; but to the righteous good shall be repaid." Chap. xiv. 32. "The wicked is driven away in his wickedness; but the righteous hath hope in his death." Chap. xvi. 4. "The Lord hath made all things for himself; yea, even the wicked for the day of evil." Chap. xxi. 12. "God overthroweth the wicked for their wickedness." Eccl. viii. 12, 13. "Though a sinner do evil an hundred times," or years, "and his days be prolonged; yet surely, I know that it shall be well with them that fear God; but it shall not be well with the wicked, neither shall he prolong his days, which are as a shadow; because he feareth not before God."

It is certain that all these evils which are denounced against the wicked, by which they are to be distinguished from the righteous, are inflicted, not in this life, but in a future state; because the same inspired writer says, there is no such distinction in this life. Eccl. ix. 1, 2. "No man knoweth either love or hatred, by all that is before them. All things come alike to all, there is one event to the righteous and to the wicked; to the good and to the clean, and to the unclean; to him that sacrificeth, and to him that sacrificeth not: As is the good, so is the sinner; and he that sweareth, as he that feareth an oath."

The

The prophet Isaiah speaks much of the dreadful evil, and unavoidable punishment, that will attend the wicked in the future state. He seems to sum up and declare the whole import of his commission and prophecy, Chap. iii. 10, 11. "Say ye to the righteous, that it shall be well with him; for they shall eat the fruit of their doings. Wo unto the wicked, it shall be ill with him; for the reward of his hands shall be given him." Here the righteous and the wicked are set in opposition to each other, with respect to the fruit and end of what they do in this world. And if what is promised to the former, be endless life and happiness; can the threatning of the contrary, to the latter, be any thing but directly the opposite, endless misery and punishment? That punishment must be very dreadful, which is a full reward of all that the sinner does in this life, that is, answerable to his ill desert: And doubtless will be without end; which will be particularly considered in the sequel.

Chap. xxviii. 16, &c. " Therefore, thus saith the Lord God, Behold I lay in Zion for a foundation, a stone, a tried stone, a precious corner stone, a sure foundation: He that believeth shall not make haste. Judgment also will I lay to the line, and righteousness to the plummet, and the hail shall sweep away the refuge of lies, and the waters shall overflow the hiding-place. And your covenant with death shall be disannulled,

and

and your agreement with hell shall not stand; when the overflowing scourge shall pass through, then shall ye be trodden down by it, &c." This passage respects Christ, and points out the certain opposite consequences of believing on him, and rejecting him. To him who believeth, the most perfect security from all evil is promised. He shall be out of the reach of the rising floods of water, and the overflowing scourge. But all the rest shall have judgment without mercy, and be punished according to their crimes, and swept away by the irresistible billows, and overflowing scourge, of the divine vengeance and wrath! What a striking, awful representation is this of the future punishment of the wicked! Chap. xxxiii. 14. "The sinners in Zion are afraid, fearfulness hath surprised the hypocrites: Who among us shall dwell with devouring fire? Who among us shall dwell with everlasting burnings?" How can this representation be just or true, if a most dreadful punishment, yea, an endless one, does not await all those sinners and hypocrites, who sustain this character to the end of life? Chap. xxxiv. 8, 9, 10. "For it is the day of the Lord's vengeance, and the year of recompences for the controversy of Zion. And the streams thereof shall be turned into pitch, and the dust thereof into brimstone, and the land thereof shall become burning pitch. It shall not be quenched night nor day, the smoke thereof shall go up forever; from generation

ration to generation it shall lie waste: None shall pass through it forever and ever."

The prophet in this passage, and in the preceding verses, is representing the dreadful punishment that shall come on the enemies of God and his church, when he shall rise up to take vengeance on them, and recompence them for their evil deeds. And when he brings into view the great evils, and awful destruction that shall come on the enemies of God's people, upon the introduction of the happy state of the church in this world, he extends this view to their misery in the future state, in which their punishment shall issue, and be completed. This is not the only instance of this kind; but we often find in the prophecies both of the prosperity and happiness of God's church and people, and the overthrow and punishment of his enemies, that the prophetic vision connects the complete and eternal happiness of the former with their happy state in this world, and includes both in the same figurative representation; and in the same manner represents the punishment of the latter. And that this passage hath reference to the future misery of the wicked, is further evident from the plain allusion to it in the Revelation, when speaking of the future and dreadful misery of the enemies of God and his people. Chap. xiv. 11. "And they shall be tormented with fire and brimstone; and the smoke of their torment ascendeth up forever and ever; and they have no rest day nor night." In

In the I. chap. of Ifai. the laſt verſe, there is another threatning of future evil to the wicked. "Behold all ye that kindle a fire, and compaſs yourſelves about with ſparks: Walk in the light of your fire, and in the ſparks that ye have kindled. This ſhall ye have of mine hand, ye ſhall lie down in ſorrow." Chap. lxiii. 1----6. "Who is this that cometh from Edom, with died garments from Bozrah? Who is glorious in his apparel, travelling in the greatneſs of his ſtrength? I that ſpeak in righteouſneſs, mighty to ſave. Wherefore art thou red in thine apparel, and thy garments like him that treadeth in the wine-fat? I have trodden the wine-preſs alone, and of the people there was none with me: For I will tread them in mine anger, and trample them in my fury, and their blood ſhall be ſprinkled upon my garments, and I will ſtain all my raiment. For the day of vengeance is in mine heart, and the year of my redeemed is come. And I will tread down the people in mine anger, and make them drunk in my fury, and I will bring down their ſtrength to the earth." Here Chriſt is repreſented as pouring vengeance on all his enemies, while he redeems and ſaves his church. This is exactly agreeable to ſeveral paſſages already quoted, and to the general current of ſcripture. The acceptable year of the Lord is, alſo, the day of vengeance of our God, Iſai. lxi. 2. And agreeable to the ſcripture now under conſideration, it is ſaid of

E   Chriſt

Christ, Rev. xix. 15. "He treadeth the wine press of the fierceness and wrath of Almighty God." And we are told by Christ himself, and by St. Paul, how, and when, this shall be completely done. Matth. xxv. 41. "Then shall he say unto them on his left hand, Depart from me, ye cursed, into everlasting fire." 2 Thess. i. 7, &c. "When the Lord Jesus shall be revealed from heaven, with his mighty angels, in flaming fire, taking vengeance on them that know not God, and that obey not the Gospel of our Lord Jesus Christ; who shall be punished with everlasting destruction from the presence of the Lord, and the glory of his power."

Isai. lxvi. 23, 24. "And it shall come to pass, that from one new moon to another, and from one sabbath to another, shall all flesh come to worship before me, saith the Lord. And they shall go forth, and look upon the carcases of the men that have transgressed against me; for their worm shall not die, neither shall their fire be quenched, and they shall be an abhorring unto all flesh."

This prophet had dwelt much on the certain overthrow and destruction of all the enemies of the church, and the prosperity and happiness to which that shall be brought in the latter days; and now concludes his prophecy in these remarkable words, which, in figurative language, represent the eternal state of the church, and of her enemies, which are destroyed and punished

for

for their transgression. Dead bodies which are not buried, soon become very nauseous and abominable, until they are wholly consumed by worms, or by fire. Here the greatness and duration of the punishment of these transgressors, is set forth by their bodies, though putrid and very offensive, continuing unconsumed by the worm, or by the fire, and remaining food for the one, and fuel for the other, without any end or diminution. And this is to take place in the sight of all the inhabitants of heaven; and they shall have it full in view, while they worship and praise God. This is exactly agreeable to other passages of scripture; especially Rev. xiv. 10. " And he shall be tormented with fire and brimstone, *in the presence of the holy angels, and in the presence of the Lamb*: And the smoke of their torment ascendeth up forever and ever." Chap. xix. 3. " And I heard a great voice of much people in heaven, saying, Alleluia; salvation, and glory, and honor, and power unto the Lord our God. And again they said, Alleluia. And her smoke rose up forever and ever." No similitude, no words, could be chosen, that would, in a more determinate and striking manner, set forth the dreadfulness and perpetuity of the future punishment of the wicked, than these used by the prophet Isaiah. For this reason, doubtless, our Saviour alludes to this passage, repeatedly, when he would set this awful subject in the most awakening point of
light

light. But this will be more particularly considered hereafter.

By the prophet Jeremiah, God fixeth an awful curse on those who refuse to trust in him; and pronounceth every one blessed that trusteth in the Lord. Chap. xvii. 5, &c. "Thus saith the Lord, Cursed be the man that trusteth in man, and maketh flesh his arm, and whose heart departeth from the Lord. For he shall be like the heath in the desert, and shall not see when good cometh, but shall inhabit the parched places in the wilderness, in a salt land, and not inhabited. Blessed is the man that trusteth in the Lord, and whose hope the Lord is. For he shall be as a tree planted by the waters, &c."

The curse here pronounced on the unbeliever, must intend the curse which will fall on him in the future state; for no such curse, as is here described, and opposed to the blessing pronounced on him who trusteth or believeth in God, comes on the sinner in this world: But, as Jeremiah himself says, in this world, "The way of the wicked prospereth, and they are happy that deal very treacherously." Chap. xii. 1. This curse is expressed in figurative language; but appears to be the same which is fixed by John the Baptist, and our Saviour on all unbelievers. "He that believeth not the son, shall not see life; but the wrath of God abideth on him. He that believeth not, shall be damned. Depart from me, ye *cursed*, into everlasting fire."

In the book of the prophet Ezekiel, it is often declared, that they who perfift in evil ways, through life, fhall *die*; fhall *die in their iniquity*. And on the contrary, they who turn from their evil ways, fhall *live*. See Chap. iii. xviii. xxxiii. By *dying* here cannot mean departing out of this life, by the death of the body; for the penitent and obedient die this death, as well as the obftinate finner. It muft therefore mean what is called the *fecond death*, which is to be judged according to their works, and caft into the lake of fire, where they fhall be tormented forever and ever. Rev. xx. 14.

But one text more will be mentioned in the Old-Teftament, importing the future punifhment of the wicked. And that is in Daniel, Chap. xii. 2. "And many of them that fleep in the duft of the earth fhall awake, fome to everlafting life, and fome to fhame and everlafting contempt."

WE now come to the New-Teftament, to fee what is faid there of the future punifhment of the wicked. We may juftly expect greater light on this head, in this more clear revelation of a future ftate. If, notwithftanding all that is found in the Old-Teftament, there be really no fuch punifhment, doubtlefs Chrift and his apoftles have plainly told us, that there will be no fuch evil; and have not faid a word that can be conftrued in favor of it. But if the glad tidings
proclaimed

proclaimed in the gospel, are consistent with the future punishment of those who reject it; and if a great, awfully aggravated, and endless punishment awaits them; the kind Saviour, who is full of grace and truth, and those whom he authorized to preach the whole truth, have certainly warned mankind of this, and stated the doctrine of the *wrath to come* in the most plain and determinate words.

John the baptist, who was raised up to introduce the Saviour, is not silent on this head; but publishes awful threats against the obstinately wicked, and those who reject Christ. Matth. iii. 7, &c. "When he saw many of the Pharisees and Sadducees come to his baptism, he said unto them, O generation of vipers, who hath warned you to flee *from the wrath to come*. Bring forth therefore fruits meet for repentance." Here he brings into view *wrath to come*, which could be avoided only by true repentance. "And now also the ax is laid unto the root of the trees: Therefore every tree which bringeth not forth good fruit is hewn down and *cast into the fire*. He that cometh after me is mightier than I; whose fan is in his hand, and he will thoroughly purge his floor, and gather his wheat into the garner, *but he will burn up the chaff with unquenchable fire.*" Joh. iii. 36. "He that believeth on the Son hath everlasting life; and he that believeth not the Son, shall not see life; *but the wrath of God abideth on him.*"

What

What need of going any further? The point is decided. He who introduceth the Saviour, plainly tells us what will be the consequence. They who repent and believe the gospel, shall be saved; but all who do not, are left in, at least, as bad a case, as they could be in, had there been no Saviour. *They shall not see life;* but the wrath of God ABIDETH on them; they shall be cast into unquenchable fire.

BUT what does Christ himself say? Mathew v. 22, &c. Whosoever shall say to his brother, Thou fool, shall be in danger of hell fire. Agree with thine adversary quickly, while thou art in the way with him; left at any time the adversary deliver thee to the judge, and the judge deliver thee to the officer, and thou be cast into prison. Verily I say unto thee, thou shalt by no means come out thence, till thou hast paid the uttermost farthing. And if thy right eye offend thee, pluck it out, and cast it from thee: For it is profitable for thee that one of thy members should perish, and not that thy whole body should be cast into hell. And if thy right hand offend thee, cut it off, and cast it from thee: For it is profitable for thee that one of thy members should perish, and not that thy whole body should be cast into hell. Chap. vii. 13. Enter ye in at the strait gate; for wide is the gate, and broad is the way that leadeth to destruction, and many there be which go in thereat."

at." v. 22, &c. "Many will say unto me in that day, Lord, Lord, have we not prophesied in thy name, and in thy name cast out devils, &c. And then will I profess unto them, I never knew you: Depart from me, ye that work iniquity. Every one that heareth these sayings of mine, and doth them not, shall be likened unto a foolish man, which built his house upon the sand: And the rain descended, and the floods came, and the winds blew, and beat upon that house; and it fell, and great was the fall of it." Chap. viii. 12. "But the children of the kingdom shall be cast out into outer darkness: There shall be weeping and gnashing of teeth." Chap. x. 15, "Verily I say unto you, it shall be more tolerable for the land of Sodom and Gomorrah, in the day of judgment, than for that city." v. 28. "Fear not them which kill the body, and are not able to kill the soul: But rather fear him which is able to destroy both soul and body in hell." Chap. xi. 21, &c. "Wo unto thee Chorazin! I say unto you, it shall be more tolerable for Tyre and Sidon at the day of judgment, than for you. And thou Capernaum, I say unto you, it shall be more tolerable for the land of Sodom in the day of judgment, than for thee." Math. xii. 31, 32. "Wherefore I say unto you, all manner of sin and blasphemy shall be forgiven unto men: But the blasphemy against the Holy Ghost shall not be forgiven unto men. And whosoever

speaketh

speaketh against the Holy Ghost, it shall not be forgiven him, neither in this world, nor in the world to come." Mark, iii. 29. "He that shall blaspheme against the Holy Ghost, hath never forgiveness, but is in danger of eternal damnation." Luke xii. 10. "And whosoever shall speak a word against the son of man, it shall be forgiven him: But unto him that blasphemeth against the Holy Ghost, it shall not be forgiven." There is a certain connexion between not being forgiven, and punishment, or damnation. Matth. xiii. 41, &c. "So shall it be in the end of the world. The son of man shall send forth his angels, and they shall gather out of his kingdom all things that offend, and them which do iniquity; and shall cast them into a furnace of fire: There shall be wailing and gnashing of teeth." So shall it be in the end of the world: The angels shall come forth, and sever the wicked from among the just; and shall cast them into the furnace of fire: There shall be wailing and gnashing of teeth." Chap. xvi, 25, &c. Whosoever will save his life, shall lose it. For what is a man profited, if he shall gain the whole world, and lose his own soul? Or, what shall a man give in exchange for his soul? For the son of man shall come in the glory of his Father, with his angels; and then shall he reward every man according to his works." Chap. xviii. 8, 9. "If thy hand or thy foot offend thee, cut them

them off and cast them from thee; it is better for thee to enter into life halt or maimed, rather than having two hands or two feet, to be cast into *everlasting fire*. And if thine eye offend thee, pluck it out, and cast it from thee: It is better for thee to enter into life with one eye, than having two eyes to be cast into hell fire." Chap. xxi. 44. "And whosoever shall fall on this stone, shall be broken: But on whomsoever it shall fall, it will grind him to powder." Chap. xxii. 13. "Then said the king to his servants, Bind him hand and foot, an take him away, and cast him into outer darkness: There shall be weeping and gnashing of teeth. For many are called, but few are chosen." Chap. xxiii. 14, 33. "Wo unto you, Scribes and Pharisees, hypocrites; for ye devour widows houses, and for a pretence make long prayers; therefore ye shall receive the greater damnation. Ye serpents, ye generation of vipers, how can ye escape the damnation of hell?" Chap. xxiv. 50, 51. "The Lord of that servant shall come in a day when he looketh not for him, and in an hour that he is not aware of; and shall cut him asunder, and appoint him his portion with the hypocrites: There shall be weeping and gnashing of teeth." Chap. xxv. 10, &c. "And while they went to buy, the bridegroom came, and they that were ready, went in with him to the marriage, and the door was shut. Afterward came also the other virgins, saying, Lord,

Lord, Lord, open to us. But he anſwered and ſaid, Verily I ſay unto you, I know you not. For unto every one that hath ſhall be given, and he ſhall have abundance; but from him that hath not, ſhall be taken away even that which he hath. And caſt ye the unprofitable ſervant into outer darkneſs: There ſhall be weeping and gnaſhing of teeth." Chap. xxvi. 24. "The ſon of man goeth as it is written of him: But wo unto that man by whom the ſon of man is betrayed: It had been good for that man, if he had not been born." Mark viii. 38. "Whoſoever therefore ſhall be aſhamed of me, and of my words, in this adulterous and ſinful generation; of him alſo ſhall the ſon of man be aſhamed, when he cometh in the glory of his Father, with the holy angels." Chap. ix. 43, &c. "And if thy hand offend thee, cut it off: it is better for thee to enter into life maimed, than having two hands, to go into hell, *into the fire that never ſhall be quenched:* Where their worm dieth not, and the fire is not quenched. And if thy foot offend thee, cut it off: It is better for thee to enter halt into life, than having two feet, to be caſt into hell, into the fire that never ſhall be quenched: Where their worm dieth not, and the fire is not quenched. And if thine eye offend thee, pluck it out: It is better for thee to enter into the kingdom of God with one eye, than having two eyes, to be caſt into hell fire: Where their worm dieth not, and
the

the fire is not quenched." Chap. xvi. 16. "He that believeth not, shall be damned." Luke, vi. 24, 25. "Wo unto you that are rich: For ye have received your consolation. Wo unto you that are full: For ye shall hunger. Wo unto you that laugh now: For ye shall mourn and weep." Chap. xii. 5, &c. "But I will forewarn you whom you shall fear, Fear him which, after he hath killed, hath power to cast into hell: Yea, I say unto you, fear him. But if that servant say in his heart, My Lord delayeth his coming, &c. The Lord of that servant will come in a day when he looketh not for him, and will cut him in sunder, and appoint him his portion with the unbelievers. And that servant which knew his Lord's will, and prepared not himself, neither did according to his will, shall be beaten with many stripes. When thou goest with thine adversary to the magistrate, as thou art in the way, give diligence that thou mayest be delivered from him; lest he hale thee to the judge, and the judge deliver thee to the officer, and the officer cast thee into prison. I tell thee, thou shalt not depart thence, till thou hast paid the very last mite." Chap. xiii. 25, &c. "When once the master of the house is risen up, and hath shut to the door, and ye begin to stand without, and to knock at the door, saying, Lord, Lord, open unto us, he shall say, I tell you, I know you not; depart from me, all ye workers of iniquity.

quity. There shall be weeping and gnashing of teeth when ye shall see Abraham, Isaac, and Jacob, and all the prophets in the kingdom of God, and you yourselves thrust out." Chap. xvi. 22, &c. "The rich man, also died, and was buried. And in hell he lift up his eyes, being in torments, and seeth Abraham afar off, and Lazarus in his bosom. And he cried, and said, Father Abraham, have mercy on me, and send Lazarus, that he may dip the tip of his finger in water, and cool my tongue; for I am tormented in this flame. But Abraham said, son, remember that thou in thy life time receivedst thy good things, and likewise Lazarus evil things: But now he is comforted, and thou art tormented. And besides all this, between us and you there is a great gulph fixed; so that they which would pass from hence to you cannot; neither can they pass to us, that would come from thence." John iii. 14, 15, 16, "And as Moses lifted up the serpent in the wilderness, even so must the son of man be lifted up; that whosoever believeth in him, *should not perish*, but have eternal life. For God so loved the world, that he gave his only begotten son, that whosoever believeth in him, *should not perish*, but have everlasting life." In these words it is implied, that they who believe not on Christ shall *perish*; and perishing is directly opposed to having everlasting life. All is implied here which is expresly asserted in v. 36, "He that believeth not

not the fon, fhall not fee life; but the wrath of God abideth on him." Chap. v. 28, 29. "The hour is coming, in which all that are in the graves fhall hear his voice, and fhall come forth; they that have done good, unto the refurrection of life; and they that have done evil, *unto the refurrection of damnation.*" Chap. viii. 21, 24. " I go my way, and ye fhall feek me, *and fhall die in your fins.* Ye are of this world, I am not of this world. I faid therefore unto you, *that ye fhall die in your fins*: For if ye believe not that I am he, *ye fhall die in your fins.*" What Chrift repeatedly threatens in thefe words, muft be evil that would come on them after their death, which can be no lefs than a proper punifhment for their fins. Chap. xii. 25, 48. "He that loveth his life, fhall lofe it: And he that hateth his life in this world, fhall keep it unto life eternal." Lofing his life, is an evil which is oppofed to keeping it to life eternal; therefore muft mean eternal death. " He that rejecteth me, and receiveth not my words, hath one that judgeth him: The word that I have fpoken, the fame fhall judge him in the laft day." That is, he fhall then be condemned and punifhed. Chap. xv. 6. " If a man abide not in me, he is caft forth as a branch, and is withered; and men gather them, and caft them into the fire, and they are burned." Matth. xxv. 41, 46. " Then fhall he fay unto them on the left hand, Depart from me, ye curfed, into everlafting

fire

fire, prepared for the devil and his angels. And these shall go away into everlasting punishment."

Who can read all these words of Christ, and yet think that he came into the world with a design to save all men from future punishment? If we had nothing but his own declarations to determine us, these are more than sufficient to give us as much assurance, that the wicked will be punished to a great and awful degree in a future state, as we can have that he is the son of God, the saviour of the world; yea, we cannot doubt of the former, without calling the latter equally in question. No person that ever spoke on earth by divine inspiration, has said so much of the future punishment of the wicked, and preached hell and damnation so much, and so often, or set it in so awful and shocking a light, as did the only begotten son of God, who is full of grace and truth.

But what we find in the writings of the apostles of Christ, will shew how they understood him on this point, and strengthen the evidence of the destruction and punishment of the wicked, in a future state, if it be capable of receiving any addition.

Act. iii. 23. "And it shall come to pass, that *every soul* which will not hear that prophet, shall be destroyed from among the people." These words, with the foregoing, are a quotation from Moses, made by the apostle Peter, in

his

his speech to the people in the temple; which words he applies to Christ, as being the prophet of which God speaks by Moses; and here is a threatning of certain destruction to every soul who shall disregard this prophet. Chap. xiii. 40, 41. "Beware therefore, lest that come upon you, which is spoken of in the prophets, Behold, ye despisers, and wonder and perish." Chap. xxiv. 25. And as he reasoned of righteousness, temperance, and judgment to come, Felix *trembled*." What could there be in Paul's preaching to make Felix tremble, if he brought no evil into view, as coming on the unrighteous and intemperate, at, and after the day of judgment? If he had preached to this wicked Roman governor, that there was no future punishment to be feared: Yea, if he had not preached the contrary, Felix could not have been terrified. Paul brought the day of judgment into view, as matter of great terror to wicked men; therefore *he* preached that they would then be condemned, and punished according to their evil deeds in this life. This appears from the words under consideration; and also from St. Paul's own words, 2 Cor. v. 10, 11. "For we must all appear before the judgment seat of Christ, that every one may receive the things done in the body, according to that he hath done, whether it be good or bad. *Knowing therefore the terror of the Lord, we persuade men.*" What words can more expressly prefsly declare, that they who die impenitent in their sins, shall, at the day of judgment, be condemned by Christ, to a punishment answerable to the number and magnitude of the crimes, of which they were guilty in this life? And this was the terror which the apostles had in view; by displaying which, they sought to perswade men to fly from the wrath to come. They who believe the wicked will not be punished after the day of judgment, do not know the terror of Christ, of which St. Paul here speaks; but deny that there is any such terror. And were a Felix to hear them preach, and believe what they say, he would be so far from *trembling*, that he would be soothed into perfect security.

But let us proceed, and see what this apostle says further of future punishment. Rom. i. 18. " For the wrath of God is revealed from heaven, against all ungodliness, and unrighteousness of men, who hold the truth in unrighteousness." Chap. ii. 5, &c. " But after thy hardness and impenitent heart, treasurest up unto thyself *wrath, against the day of wrath*, and revelation of the righteous judgment of God. Who will render to every man according to his deeds. Unto them that are contentious, and do not obey the truth, but obey unrighteousness; *indignation and wrath, tribulation and anguish*, upon every soul of man that doth evil. For as many as have sinned without law, *shall perish* without law: And as many as have sinned in the law, shall be judged

by the law; in the day when God shall judge the secrets of men by Jesus Christ, according to my gospel." Chap. viii. 13. "For if ye live after the flesh, *ye shall die.*" That is the second death, which is the wages of sin, in opposition to eternal life. "For the wages of sin is death; but the gift of God is eternal life, through Jesus Christ our Lord." Chap. ix. 22. "What if God, willing to shew his wrath, and make his power known, endured with much long suffering the vessels of wrath, fitted to destruction." 1 Cor. i. 18. with 2 Cor. ii. 15, 16. "For the preaching of the cross is *to them that perish* foolishness: But unto us which are saved, it is the power of God. For we are unto God a sweet favour of Christ, in them that are saved, and *in them that perish.* To the one we are a savour of death unto death; and to the other a savour of life unto life." 1 Cor. iii. 17. "If any man defile the temple of God, *him shall God destroy.*" Chap. ix. 27. "But I keep under my body, and bring it into subjection; lest that by any means, when I have preached to others, *I myself should be a castaway.*" Gal. vi 7, 8. "Be not deceived; God is not mocked: For whatsoever a man soweth, that shall he reap. For he that soweth to the flesh, shall of the flesh reap corruption: but he that soweth to the spirit, shall of the spirit reap life everlasting." Eph. v. 5, 6. "For this ye know, that no whoremonger, nor unclean person, nor covetous man, hath any inheritance

heritance in the kingdom of Chrift, and of God. Let no man deceive you with vain words: *For becaufe of thefe things cometh the wrath of God upon the children of difobedience.*" Phil. i. 28. " And in nothing terrified by your adverfaries: Which is to them an evident token *of perdition;* but to you of falvation, and that of God." Chap. iii. 18, 19. " For many walk, of whom I have told you often, and now tell you, even weeping, that they are the enemies of the crofs of Chrift: *whofe end is deftruction.*" Col. iii. 5, 6. " Mortify therefore your members which are upon the earth, fornication, covetoufnefs, &c. for which things fake, *the wrath of God cometh on the children of difobedience.*" v. 25. " But he that doth wrong, *fhall receive for the wrong which he hath done;* And there is no refpect of perfons." 1 Theff. i. 10. " Whom he raifed from the dead, even Jefus, *which delivered us from the wrath to come.*" Chap. iv. 6. " That no man go beyond and defraud his brother in any matter; *becaufe the Lord is the avenger of all fuch,* as we alfo have forewarned you, and teftified." Chap. v. 3. " For when they fhall fay, peace and fafety; then fudden deftruction cometh upon them, as travail upon a woman with child: *And they fhall not efcape.*" 2 Theff. i. 6, 7, 8, 9. " Seeing it is a righteous thing with God to recompenfe tribulation to them that trouble you; and to you who are *troubled,* reft with us, when the Lord Jefus fhall be

revealed

revealed from heaven, with his mighty angels, in flaming fire, taking vengeance on them that know not God, and that obey not the gospel of our Lord Jesus Christ: Who shall be punished with everlasting destruction from the presence of the Lord, and the glory of his power." Chap. ii. 10, 11, 12. "And with all deceivableness of unrighteousness, *in them that perish*; because they received not the love of the truth, that they might be saved. And for this cause God shall send them strong delusion, that they should believe a lie: *That they all might be damned*, who believed not the truth, but had pleasure in unrighteousness." 1 Tim, v. 24. "Some mens sins are open before hand, *going before to judgment*; and some men they follow after." Chap. vi. 9. "But they that will be rich fall into temptation, and a snare, and into many foolish and hurtful lusts, *which drown men in destruction and perdition*." 2. Tim. ii. 12. "If we suffer, we shall also reign with him: If we deny him, *he also will deny us*." Heb. ii. 2, 3. "For if the word spoken by angels was stedfast, and every transgression and disobedience received a just recompence of reward; how shall we escape, if we neglect so great salvation?" Chap. iii. 19. compared with iv. 11. "So we see that they could not enter in because of unbelief. Let us labour therefore to enter into that rest, lest any man fall after the same example of unbelief." Chap. vi. 4, &c. "For it is impossible for those

who

who were once enlightened, &c.—If they shall fall away, to renew them again unto repentance: Seeing they crucify to themselves the Son of God afresh, and put him to an open shame. For the earth, which drinketh in the rain that cometh oft upon it, and bringeth forth herbs, &c. receiveth blessing from God. But that which beareth thorns and briars, is rejected, and is nigh unto cursing: Whose end is to be burned." Chap. x. 26, &c. "For if we sin wilfully after that we have received the knowledge of the truth, there remaineth no more sacrifice for sins: But a certain fearful looking for of judgment, and fiery indignation, which shall devour the adversaries. He that despised Moses's law died without mercy: *Of how much sorer punishment, suppose ye, shall he be thought worthy,* who hath trodden under foot the Son of God, and counted the blood of the covenant, wherewith he was sanctified, an unholy thing; and hath done despite to the Spirit of Grace? For we know him that hath said, Vengeance belongeth unto me, I will recompense, saith the Lord. It is a fearful thing to fall into the hands of the living God! But we are not of them who draw back *unto perdition*; but of them that believe, to the saving of the soul." Chap. xii. 15, &c. " Looking diligently, lest any man fail of the grace of God; lest any root of bitterness springing up, trouble you, and thereby many be defiled: Lest there be any fornicator, -

tor, or profane perfon, as Efau, who for one morfel of meat fold his birthright. For ye know how that afterward, when he would have inherited the bleffing, he was rejected: For he found no place of repentance, though he fought it carefully, with tears. See that ye refufe not him that fpeaketh: For if they efcaped not who refufed him that fpake on earth, *much more fhall not we efcape*, if we turn away from him that fpeaketh from heaven."

We have alfo the apoftle James's witnefs to future punifhment. Jam. ii. 13. "For he fhall have judgment without mercy, that hath fhewed no mercy." To have judgment without mercy, is to be punifhed according to his ill defert. Jam. iv. 12. "There is one lawgiver, who is able to fave, *and to deftroy:* Who art thou that judgeft another?" Jam. v. 1, &c. "Go to now, ye rich men, weep and howl *for your miferies that fhall come upon you.* Your gold and your filver is cankered; and the ruft of them fhall be a witnefs againft you, and fhall eat your flefh, as it were fire: *Ye have heaped treafure together for the laft days.*"

St. Peter comes next in courfe. 1. Pet. iii. 19. "By which alfo he went and preached to the fpirits in prifon; which fometime were difobedient, when once the long fuffering of God waited in the days of Noah, while the ark was preparing." Here the fpirits of the finners of the old world, to whom Noah preached, being

influenced

influenced thereto by the spirit of Christ, are spoken of as being in prison, when St. Peter wrote, which was above 2000 years after they left this world. They are therefore prisoners *now*, confined in darkness and despair, to the judgment of the great day. Chap. iv. 17, 18. " For the time is come that judgment must begin at the house of God: And if it first begin at us, *what shall be the end of them that obey not the gospel of God?* And if the righteous scarcely be saved, *where shall the ungodly and the sinner appear?*" Chap. v. 8. " Be sober, be vigilant; because your adversary, the devil, as a roaring lion, walketh about *seeking whom he may devour*." 2. Pet. ii. 1, 3, &c. " *Who bring on themselves swift destruction*. Whose judgment now of a long time lingereth not, and *their damnation slumbereth not*. For if God spared not the angels that sinned, but cast them down to hell, and delivered them into chains of darkness, to be reserved unto judgment, and spared not the old world, bringing in the flood upon the world of the ungodly; and turning the cities of Sodom and Gomorrah into ashes, condemned them with an overthrow, making them an example unto those that after should live ungodly; the Lord knoweth how to reserve the unjust *unto the day of judgment, to be punished*. These, as natural brute beasts, made to be taken and destroyed, *shall utterly perish* in their corruption. These are wells without water, clouds that are

carried

carried with a tempeſt, *to whom the miſt of darkneſs is reſerved forever.*" Chap. iii. 7, 9, 16. "But the heavens and the earth which are now, by the ſame word are kept in ſtore, reſerved unto fire againſt the day of judgment, *and perdition of ungodly men.* The Lord is not ſlack concerning his promiſe (as ſome men count ſlackneſs) but is long-ſuffering to us-ward, not willing that any ſhould periſh, but that all ſhould come to repentance." Here it is ſuppoſed that all will periſh, who do not come to repentance in this life, while God waits on them; and therefore certain deſtruction to thoſe who continue impenitent through life, under all means uſed with them to bring them to repentance, is in theſe words fully aſſerted.

It will be thought ſtrange, perhaps, by ſome, that this paſſage, from which it has been inferred that all mankind will be ſaved, ſhould be uſed to prove directly the reverſe, viz. that many will periſh. It has been ſaid, if God is not willing that any ſhould periſh, certainly none can periſh; for who hath reſiſted his will?

To this it may be anſwered, in the firſt place, That it is certainly very ſtrange indeed, and perfectly unaccountable, that St. Peter ſhould here aſſert that none of mankind will periſh; ſince he had declared the contrary, over and over again, in this epiſtle; and does it even in this very paragraph. He had ſaid, that falſe teachers would bring on themſelves *ſwift deſtruction.*

struction. That God referved the wicked to the day of judgment, *to be punished.* That they shall *utterly* PERISH in their own corruption. And in the next verfe but one before this, fays, the heavens and the earth are referved unto fire, againft the day of judgment, *and perdition of ungodly men.* And with reference to this awful cataftrophe, he fays, that God does not bring it on immediately, becaufe he is long fuffering, and difpofed to give men time and opportunity to repent, not willing that any fhould perifh in that deftruction, which he had juft faid was coming on ungodly men. So that he here afferts, God is longfuffering, not willing that any fhould perifh, as he had juft faid ungodly men will perifh; for whofe perdition God had already made provifion.

The way is now prepared to anfwer, in the next place. When the apoftle fays, God is longfuffering, not willing that any fhould perifh, but that all fhould come to repentance, the natural, plain, and only confiftent meaning is, that God in his dealings with men, in his providence, does not confult and purfue methods to circumvent and enfnare them, to prevent their having a fufficient and fair opportunity to repent; but puts them under all proper advantages for this; fets before them the ftrongeft motives, and waits upon them with great patience and long fuffering; and who has at the fame time declared, that if they do not come to

repentance

repentance in this life, they shall certainly perish in the perdition of ungodly men. He will not put an end to the world, until he has used all proper and suitable means, and taken the greatest conceivable variety of methods and ways, in the wisest and best manner, adapted to bring them to repentance; that they who continue impenitent may appear in their true obstinacy, and perverseness and be left wholly without any excuse; and their full desert of the destruction which God will bring upon them, and his righteousness in punishing them, may be seen in the clearest light, by all.

And, by the way, they who suppose that St. Peter here asserts, that not one shall perish, must allow he equally asserts, that all shall come to repentance; for God is said to will the latter, as much as the former. And this repentance is to take place in this life; because God is long-suffering towards them in this world, for this end. But they do not pretend, that God brings all men, to repentance in this world. If then, notwithstanding what God wills respecting their repentance, they do not repent; what evidence is there that they will not perish? If they say, the repentance which God wills, is to take place in the other world; it will then be asked, Why he is long suffering toward them *in this world*, in order to their coming to repentance *in the other world*? If they are not to come to repentance in this life, why does God wait upon on them here, even to long suffering, and not send them directly into the other world, where they will repent? For to wait on them here, is only to put their repentance off to a greater distance. To send them out of this world, is the only way to effect and hasten their repentance.

But to proceed,—This apostle speaks of those who go to destruction by abusing the holy scriptures. "In which, i. e. St. Paul's writings, are some things hard to be understood, which they that are unlearned (or rather *unteachable)* and unstable wrest, as they do also the other scriptures, *unto their own destruction.*"

The apostle Jude speaks in much the same language with St. Peter, of the punishment and destruction of sinners. He says "I will therefore put you in remembrance how that the Lord, having saved the people out of the land of Egypt, afterwards *destroyed* them that beleived not. And the angels which kept not their first estate, but left their own habitation, he hath reserved in everlasting chains, under darkness, unto the judgment of the great day; even as Sodom and Gomorrah, and the cities about them, are set forth for an example, *suffering the vengeance of eternal fire.* Likewise these filthy dreamers, &c.—Wo unto them, for they have gone in the way of Cain, and ran greedily in the way of Balaam for a reward, and *perished* in the gainsaying of Corah. These are wandering stars, *to whom is reserved the blackness of darkness forever.*" The

Sect. I.

The apostle John, who so much celebrates the love of God, yet speaks of future punishment. 1 John. v. 16. "There is a sin unto death: I do not say that he shall pray for it." That is, there is a sin which God will not pardon; but it is infallibly connected with the second death, which is the wages of sin. I therefore do not direct any christian to pray for the pardon of this sin. But more of this is to be found in the book of the Revelation, written by St. John. Chap. ii. 11. "He that overcometh *shall not be hurt of the second death.* It is here implied, that all who do not overcome in this life, shall suffer the second death. What this is, we shall find fully explained in this book, Chap. xi. 18. "And the nations were angry, *and thy wrath is come,* and the time of the dead, that they should be judged, and that thou shouldest give reward unto thy servants; *and shouldest destroy them which destroy the earth.*" The destruction here spoken of is consequent on the day of judgment. Chap. xiv. 9, &c. "And the third angel followed them, saying with a loud voice, If any man worship the beast and his image, and receive his mark in his forehead, or in his hand, the same *shall drink of the wine of the wrath of God, which is poured out without mixture, into the cup of his indignation: And he shall be tormented with fire and brimstone,* in the presence of the holy angels, and in the presence of the Lamb. *And the smoke of their torment ascendeth up forever and*

and ever: And they have no reſt day nor night. And the angel thruſt in his ſickle into the earth, and gathered the vine of the earth, and caſt it into *the great wine-preſs of the wrath of God.* And the wine-preſs was trodden without the city, and blood came out of the wine-preſs, even unto the horſe-bridles, by the ſpace of a thouſand and ſix hundred furlongs." Chap. xix. 1, 3, " And I heard a great voice of much people in heaven, ſaying, Alleluia : Salvation, and glory, and honor, and power unto the Lord our God. And again they ſaid, Alleluia. *And her ſmoke roſe up forever and ever.*" Chap. xx. 6, &c. " Bleſſed and holy is he that hath part in the firſt reſurrection : *On ſuch the ſecond death hath no power.* And fire came down from God out of heaven, and devoured them. And the devil that deceived them, was caſt into the lake of fire and brimſtone, where the beaſt and the falſe prophet are : *And ſhall be tormented day and night, forever and ever.* And I ſaw a great white throne, and him that ſat on it. And I ſaw the dead, ſmall and great, ſtand before God. And they were judged every man according to their works. And death and hell were caſt into the lake of fire. THIS IS THE SECOND DEATH. And whoſoever was not found written in the book of life, was caſt into the lake of fire." Chap. xxi. 8. " But the fearful, and unbelieving, and the abominable, and murderers, and whoremongerers, and ſorcerers,

Sect. I.

cerers, and idolaters, and all liars, shall have their part in the lake that burneth with fire and brimstone: *Which is the second death.* Ch. xxii. 10, &c. "And he said unto me, seal not the sayings of the prophecy of this book: For the time is at hand. He that is unjust, *let him be unjust still;* and he which is filthy, *let him be filthy still*: And he that is righteous, let him be righteous still: And he that is holy let him be holy still. And behold I come quickly; and my reward is with me, *to give every man according as his work shall be.* Blessed are they that do his commandments, that they may have right to the tree of life, and may enter in through the gates into the city. For without are dogs and sorcerers, and whoremongers, and idolaters, and whosoever loveth and maketh a lie. I testify unto every man that heareth the words of the prophecy of this book, If any man shall add unto these things, *God shall add unto him the plagues that are written in this book.* And if any man shall take away from the words of the book of this prophecy, God shall take away his part out of the book of life, and out of the holy city, and from the things which are written in this book. He which testifieth these things, saith, surely I come quickly, Amen."

Having thus attended to what we find in the holy scriptures, respecting the future punishment of the wicked, the following remarks may be made upon it. 1. Their

1. Their punishment will certainly be very great and terrible. If it were not so, there would not be so much said of it, and it would not be represented in such language, and by such figures and similitudes, as have been transcribed. It is said, they shall be cast into a furnace of fire, where they shall express their anguish, torture and rage, by wailing and gnashing of teeth. They shall be tormented day and night, without cessation, or the least intermission of ease, in a lake of fire and brimstone. They shall suffer God's fiery indignation and wrath, being in the utmost tribulation and anguish: And in punishing them God will shew his wrath, and make his power known; they being vessels of wrath, fitted to this terrible destruction, &c. &c. That must be a very great and dreadful evil which requires such language as this, in order to give us the most proper idea of it, that we can have in this state?

2. It is abundantly evident, from a great number of the passages of scripture which have been cited, that this punishment is to be extended beyond the day of judgment; yea, will then commence in its proper magnitude, and terrible perfection. They are said to be *reserved unto the day of judgment, to be punished.* They are said to be treasuring up wrath, while in this world, against that day of wrath: And *then* they are to receive the awful sentence from Christ, *Depart, ye cursed, into everlasting fire,* and actually *go away into everlasting punishment.* 3. Is

3. Is it not surprising, that any who profess to adhere to the bible as a revelation from God, should believe there is no punishment for the wicked in a future state; or if there may be some degree of evil after death, it will not be extended beyond the day of judgment, in any instance; but all will be perfectly happy from that time, forever! This notion is so directly opposed to the scripture account of this matter; and particularly the passages which have been now mentioned; that it may be expected they, especially the most sensible of them, who have embraced it, will either soon give it up, and admit that the wicked will be punished in the future state, after the day of judgment; or reject the bible, and turn deists. If they do the latter, they will be more consistent with themselves, than now they are. If they persist in their present professed belief, with the bible in their hands, they must be considered as remarkable instances of infatuation, and "strong delusion." They indeed say, they have a number of passages of scripture in favour of their opinion. But he who has with seriousness and attention considered the scriptures which have been now produced, may be confident, that no scripture can be found to support a doctrine so directly contrary to such a great number of plain, express declarations. And that he must be under the power of great prejudice, and enthusiasm, who can be confident he has found

one

one paſſage in favour of ſuch a doctrine. However, the ſcriptures they produce will be particularly conſidered hereafter; by which, it is hoped, the juſtice of this remark will be ſufficiently ſupported. *

4. It

* To evade the force of the numerous declarations and threatnings of the future puniſhment of the wicked, which have been recited in the foregoing pages, they who deny that any man will be puniſhed in the future ſtate, have ſuggeſted the following things.

It has been ſaid, *Theſe threatnings are all leveled againſt the ſins of men; and that theſe ſins or evil principles in men, when ſeparated from them, ſhall be puniſhed.*

But to talk of the exiſtence and puniſhment, pain and ſufferings of ſins or evil principles in men, when ſeparated from thoſe who ſinned, and they are made perfectly happy, is too abſurd and ridiculous to need a ſerious and formal anſwer. And it is difficult to conceive how any *man* can be ſatisfied with ſuch a ſolution; or even *believe* what he advances.

It has alſo been ſaid, *That this threatened puniſhment is to be inflicted on the devils, not on man.*

Anſwer. Though this does not ſhock common ſenſe ſo much as that juſt mentioned; yet, it flatly contradicts what is expreſſed in every threatning; for *wicked men* are threatened, not devils. It undermines all ground of reliance on the word of God; for according to this, when he ſays, hundreds of times, that *wicked men* ſhall be puniſhed, and particularly gives their character, he does not mean any ſuch thing! Beſides, when the devil ſhall be caſt into the lake of fire, the beaſt and falſe prophet are there with him, where they ſhall be tormented forever and ever. Yea, all the fearful and unbelieving, and murderers, and whoremongers, ſorcerers, idolaters, and all liars, ſhall have their part in the ſame lake of fire. Rev. xx. 10. xxi. 8.

Others have ſaid, *Theſe threatnings are deſigned only to ſhew what ſinners deſerve; and not what they ſhall ſuffer: For Chriſt ſuffers the whole; all the evil threatened falls on him. The ſinner therefore will eſcape, what he otherwiſe muſt have ſuffered.*

Anſwer.

4. It ought to be observed, that though these scriptures have been produced, only to shew, that it is abundantly asserted, that a sore and awful punishment awaits all the wicked in the future

Answer 1. This is directly contrary to those threatnings and declarations. It is expressly said, in a great variety of passages, that *wicked men*, whose character is particularly and abundantly described, shall themselves, in their own persons, be punished; that God will inflict it on *them*; and that *these* shall be rewarded according to their works, and receive of Christ the judge, according to what they have done in the body; and that these shall actually go away into everlasting punishment, &c. &c.

Answer 2. If those declarations and threatnings were only to declare and shew, what *all men* deserve, and not what any will suffer: Or if they all refer to Christ, and he is the only person that suffers; then one man, or class of men, of a particular character, could not be pointed out as the objects of these declarations and threatnings, more than all others; for, on this supposition, they must be equally true of all men, and equally applicable to them, whatever be their character: Why then is this punishment threatened, and said to be inflicted only on one class of men, of a particular character, viz. Those who have no love to Christ, are unbelievers, know not God, and do not obey the gospel, &c. While not one threatning, but promises of deliverance and salvation, are made to those of a different and contrary character; and it is abundantly declared, that while the former are punished with everlasting destruction, the latter shall not be punished, or condemned, but have everlasting life? This is impossible!

On the whole, do not such notions and evasions as these, serve to shew how weak and defenceless their cause is, who assert there is no punishment for any man in the world to come, rather than to give it so much as any plausible support? Surely they tend to render the bible useless and contemptible. Must not every consistent friend to that sacred book, reject them with abhorrance; and not without surprise, that they should be ever thought of, by any man?

future state, who die impenitent; yet, from an attentive view of them, they prove *more*, even that this punishment will be without end. This has been remarked concerning a number of scriptures that have been mentioned, in which the punishment is not *expressly* said to be everlasting; but that it will be so, is necessarily implied: And the same remark might be made concerning a number of others. And it may be observed here, that what the scripture says of future punishment, being considered in one collective view; nothing can be found which carries the least intimation that this punishment will ever end: Which we might expect, since there is so much said of it, if this were true; especially, since there is such infinite difference between a temporary and an endless punishment, and it is of such importance to men to know, whether it be without end, or not: But on the contrary, the whole taken together, or if every passage be viewed separately, it carries the complexion of an endless punishment: Especially, since it is so often, and in such a particular way and connexion, asserted to be *eternal* or *everlasting*. But as this was not to be particularly considered under this head, it of course brings us to the next section.

SECTION.

SECTION II.

WHEREIN it is particularly considered, whether it be revealed in the Holy Scriptures, that the future Punishment of the Wicked will be endless.

IT is particularly and abundantly declared in the holy scriptures, that the future punishment of the wicked will have no end. The evidence of this proposition will be produced under the following particulars.

FIRST, The punishment of the wicked is many times, in the scripture, expressly declared to be everlasting, eternal, and to continue forever.

These passages have been mentioned under the preceding head, but must be rehearsed here, with a view to illustrate this particular. Job. xx. 7. It is said, that the wicked perish *forever.* Psal. xcii. 7. "When the wicked spring as the grass, and when all the workers of iniquity do flourish, it is that they shall be destroyed *for ever.*" Isai. xxxiv. 14. The evil that is coming on sinners, is called "*everlasting burnings.*" And the prophet Daniel, speaking of the wicked, says, they shall rise to shame and *everlasting* contempt. Chap. xii. 2. St. Paul, speaking of Christ's coming to judgment, to take vengeance on all that have not known and obeyed him, says, they shall be punished with *everlasting destruction.* The apostles Peter and Jude, speaking of the punishment

punishment of the wicked, say, "To whom the mist of darknefs is referved *forever.*"— "To whom is referved the blacknefs of darknefs *forever.* Even as Sodom and Gomorrah, and the cities about them, giving themfelves over to fornication, and going after ftrange flefh, are fet forth for an example, fuffering the vengeance of *eternal fire.*" 2 Peter, ii. 17. Jude v. 7. 13. And Chrift himfelf has repeatedly declared, that the punifhment of the wicked will be *everlafting.* Mark iii. 29. "He that fhall blafpheme againft the Holy Ghoft, hath never forgivenefs, but is in danger of *eternal damnation.*" Matth. xviii. 8. "It is better for thee to *enter into life* halt or maimed, rather than having two hands or two feet, to be caft into *everlafting fire.* Matth. xxv. 41, 46. "Then fhall he fay alfo unto them on the left hand, Depart from me, ye curfed, into *everlafting fire*, prepared for the devil and his angels. And thefe fhall go away into *everlafting punifhment :* But the righteous into *life eternal.*" On the laft mentioned words, the following obfervations may be made.

1. Our Saviour here gives a particular and folemn reprefentation of the day of judgment, and ftates the iffue of it, both to the righteous and the wicked, very particularly; and doubtlefs ufes language that is quite plain and intelligible, fo that the final ftate of one and the other is precifely ftated, and will be clearly

fuggefted,

suggested, without need of any laboured criticism. The subject is of infinite importance to all: And when our divine teacher undertakes to give a particular account of it, and to tell all men, of every capacity, learned and unlearned, what are the different and opposite characters of those whom he will set on his right hand, and on his left; and what will be the sentence which he will pronounce on each; what will be the reward and happiness of the one, and what the punishment and misery of the other; we may be sure he has chosen words that are most plain and easy to be understood, and best suited to convey the truth: And has properly guarded against every mistake. He has not left us in the dark about the duration of the happiness of the righteous, or punishment of the wicked; whether the one or the other shall be endless, or infinitely short of it; but most certainly, has stated this important point, in which we are all so much interested, very precisely; so that we are in no danger of making a mistake, and of taking his meaning to be infinitely otherwise than it really is, unless it be wholly our own fault.

2. The word which our Saviour uses twice, in this passage, to denote the duration of the punishment of the wicked, and tell us how long this shall last, he has used twenty times on various occasions, and in different discourses; and in every one of these instances he evidently

ly uses it in exactly one and the same sense, and intends by it an endless duration. And when he uses it twice here on purpose to tell us how long the punishment of the wicked shall continue, is it possible that he should intend by it something infinitely different, a duration infinitely short of endless; and that without giving the least intimation of his using it in such a different sense?——So far from this, that he uses it in such a connexion here, as will naturally lead us to understand him, as designing to express an endless duration, though he had never used the word on any other occasion. This leads to another remark.

3. The same word is used here, in the very same sentence, to express the endless life and happiness of the righteous, which is used to denote the duration of the punishment of the wicked. "And these shall go away into *everlasting punishment*; but the righteous into *life eternal*." The word in our translation is indeed varied; though *everlasting* and *eternal* have precisely the same meaning; but in the original, the very *same word* is used in each part of the sentence, and might be most exactly rendered, These shall go away into *everlasting punishment*; but the righteous into *everlasting life*. If the life into which the righteous go, be endless, which all grant, and Jesus uses a word here to express such a duration; then certainly the same word, used in the same sentence, to express

the

the duration of the punishment into which the wicked shall go, must mean an endless duration: Especially, as the life of the righteous, and punishment of the wicked, are set in direct opposition to each other. If the punishment of the wicked were temporary, and must have an end; and the life of the righteous endless: So that the former is as nothing, compared with the latter; and the wicked, as well as the righteous, were equally to enjoy everlasting life; would Christ thus set the endless happiness of the righteous, and the temporary misery of the wicked, in direct opposition to each other, and in the same sentence use the same word to express a duration infinitely different? This cannot be: For such a supposition makes him confound language, as never any man did, and render it perfectly unintelligible and insignificant. This represents Him, who is full of grace and truth, and came into the world to reveal the wonderful love and grace of God, and accomplish and display the great salvation of man, as using words, and speaking, in a manner which tends to deceive men, and make them believe that this salvation is far less extensive than it really is, and lead them to think he will punish the wicked infinitely more than he designs: That the duration of this punishment will be equal to that of the happiness of the righteous, when, in truth, it is infinitely less, and not worthy to be mentioned, in comparison with the latter.

latter. This be far from him! And if it be, there is as much reason to conclude, from his most express and pointed assertion, that the punishment of the wicked will be without end, as that the happiness of the righteous will be so: Yea, we may be as sure of it, as we can be, that he is a Teacher come from God.

SECONDLY, The endless punishment of the wicked is expressed a number of times in scripture, in words yet more emphatical, if possible; when it is said to continue *forever and ever.* Rev. xiv. 10, 11. "And he shall be tormented with fire and brimstone, in the presence of the holy angels, and in the presence of the Lamb: And the smoke of their torment ascendeth up *forever and ever.*" Chap. xix. 3. "And again they said Alleluia: And her smoke rose up *forever and ever.*" Chap. xx. 10. "And the devil that deceived them, was cast into the lake of fire and brimstone, where the beast and the false prophet are; and shall be tormented day and night, *forever and ever.*" And all the wicked are said to be cast into this lake. v. 15, "And whosoever was not found written in the book of life, was cast into the lake of fire." Chap. xxi. 8. "But the fearful and unbelieving, and the abominable, and murderers, and whoremongers, and sorcerers, and idolaters, and *all liars*, shall have their part in the lake which burneth with fire and brimstone; which is the second death."

This expression, *forever and ever*, is found *twenty-two* times in the original, in the New Testament. It is used *eight* times in the epistles of St. Paul and Peter, where they ascribe glory, honor, and praise and dominion to God, *forever and ever.* It is found *fourteen* times in this book of the Revelations. It is used *twice*, to express the duration of the kingdom and reign of Christ, and the redeemed. Chap. xi. 15 "The kingdoms of this world are become the kingdoms of our Lord, and of his Christ,

Christ, and he shall reign *forever and ever.*" Chap. xxii. 5. "And there shall be no night there, and they need no candle, neither light of the sun; for the Lord God giveth them light: And *they shall reign forever and ever.*" *Three* times it is used to express the endless duration of the power, glory and dominion, of God. Chap. i. 6. "To him be glory and dominion, *forever and ever.*" v. 13. "Blessing and honor and glory, and power, be unto him that sitteth upon the throne, and unto the Lamb, *forever and ever.*" vii. 12 "Blessing, and glory, and wisdom, and thanksgiving, and honor, and power, and might, be unto our God *forever and ever.*" *Six* times it is used to express the endless existence and life of God. Chap. i. 18. "I am he that liveth, and was dead: And behold I am alive *forevermore.* The words are the same in the original, which are elsewhere translated, forever and ever. iv. 9, 10. "And when those four beasts give glory, and honor, and thanks to him that sat on the throne, *who liveth forever and ever,* the four and twenty elders fall down before him that sat on the throne, and worship him that *liveth forever and ever.*" v. 14. "And the four and twenty elders fell down and worshipped him *that liveth forever and ever.*" x. 6. "And sware by him *that liveth forever and ever.*" xv. 7. "And one of the four beasts gave unto the seven angels, seven golden vials full of the wrath of God, *who liveth forever and ever.*" The same words are used *three times,* to express the duration of the punishment of the wicked, in the places which have been quoted above.

When we find the very same words, used in the New-Testament near twenty times, to express an endless duration, and above ten times in this book of the Revelation; and six of them, most emphatically, and in the strongest manner, to mark God's eternity, or the endless duration of his existence; and at the same time, find them

them used *three times*, in the same book, by the same writer, to denote the duration of future punishment; is it possible to mistake the meaning, and think that in these *three instances* only, these words are used for a finite duration? How can any one think they do not mean an endless duration, in these places, but something infinitely short of it, without doing violence to the scripture, and his own reason?

If it were contrary to God's nature and perfections, to punish sinners with endless misery, and very impious, and most dishonorable to him; and of the worst tendency to man, for us to entertain such a thought (which they who oppose this doctrine generally assert) can it be thought, that he would express himself so, on this point, as would naturally, and even necessarily, lead all to conclude he will thus punish them, even as long as he himself shall exist, and not say a word to guard against this conclusion? Is it possible he should do this, in a revelation which is designed to give men right notions of the divine character, and of the future state of the wicked, and in the most plain and decisive manner, declare what they are to expect; and to guard against all wrong and hurtful conceptions, respecting this infinitely important subject? Most certainly, he who *liveth forever and ever*, and whose kingdom, honor and praise from the redeemed, will continue *forever and ever*, will punish his impenitent enemies *forever and ever*, even as long as he liveth. To doubt of this, is to call in question the divine authority of this Revelation.

It has been said by some, that the words *everlasting*, *forever*, and *forever and ever*, do not mean an endless duration; and are often used for a limited time in scripture: And that the words in the Hebrew and Greek languages, translated into the above English words, do not signify an endless duration: Therefore it does not
follow.

follow that the punishment of the wicked will be without end, though such words are used to denote its duration.

Whether there be any weight in this objection, let every one judge, when he has attended to the following observations.

1. It is certain that the words *eternal, everlasting, forever, &c.* are, in a great number of instances, used in the Old-testament to express the duration of the existence of God, and of his kingdom and reign, of his truth, mercy, praise and honor, and of his counsels and designs, and the happiness of his friends, &c. And in all these instances, an endless duration is intended. We are obliged to affix this meaning to these words here; and therefore without doubt this is the proper meaning of them, and they must be so understood wherever they are used, unless we are guarded against it, by an express or necessary limitation.

2. It does not yet appear, that these words are ever used in the original, when they are translated *everlasting, forever, &c.* where it would not be proper to make use of them, though they do, when considered in their proper, full meaning, signify an endless duration; but the contrary is evident. This observation might be illustrated, by producing all the instances in which these words are used in the Old-Testament; but this would be too tedious. It may suffice to mention one or two; and leave the reader to examine others, if he pleases. When it is said of a servant who refused his freedom, and consequently had his ear bored through with an awl, by his master, that he shall serve him *forever*; though the subject necessarily limits the meaning to this life; yet a word that means an endless duration is properly used here, to signify his perpetual servitude, in opposition to his being made free. When it is fre-

quently said of many of the laws which were given to Israel by Moses, that they were to be *everlasting* statutes, &c. and should be so to that peop'e; the meaning is plain, viz. That they should *never* disregard them and set them aside; and a word that signifies *endless*, is the most proper to be used in this case: And indeed no other word could convey the idea designed to be expressed. Therefore, though these words are used in instances, where the nature of the subject does in some respect limit them; yet this is no evidence that they do in themselves signify a limited time; because a word that signifies an unlimited duration, is most proper, and even necessary, to convey the idea in the most plain, and the strongest manner. *

5 As to those words in the New testament, the English reader, who knows nothing of the original Greek, may have full satisfaction about the meaning of them; and that they must intend an endless duration, even when they respect the punishment of the wicked; since they are used so often, to express the endless existence of God, and his kingdom, and the never ending life and happiness of the redeemed; and never are used for a temporary duration, unless it be in this instance; which cannot be supposed, without confounding language

---

* In a deed of conveyance of land, it is given and granted to him to whom the conveyance is made, and his heirs, *forever.* This *forever* is necessarily limited, and is not designed to extend beyond the end of the world; and yet, a word which signifies an unlimited duration, or *endless*, is the most proper word to be used here, to signify that the grantor will *never* revoke the conveyance. And if any one, observing the use of this word *forever*, in those instruments of conveyance, should hence conclude, that neither this word, nor any one in the English language, did signify an endless duration, in any case whatever, he would reason as well as they do, who make the objection above.

Sect. I.

guage, and doing violence to words, as has been observed.

4. The greek word which is used *six* times to express the duration of the punishment of the wicked, and translated *eternal* and *everlasting*, is to be found in above *seventy* places in the New-testament: And it every where is evidently used to express an endless duration, unless those six places, which speak of the duration of future punishment be excepted. And is not this sufficient to ascertain the meaning of the word, if we had no other way to determine what it is designed to express?* If a consistent

---

* This word is *aionios*, and is derived from *Aion*; which is used above *an hundred* times in the New-Testament, and does not mean any certain, definite, but an indeterminate duration, unless it be limited by the words or subject, with which it is connected. And when the preposition *eis* is put before it, whether it be used in the singular or plural number, it always signifies an endless duration, and is generally translated *forever*, and sometimes *never*; of which there are near forty instances, only two of which respect the duration of future punishment, viz. 2 Pet. ii. 17. Jude v. 13. And no reason can be given why it should not be understood here, as it must be in other places, where it is used. When the words are doubled, they are more emphatical, and are translated *forever and ever*. There are twenty-two instances of this, nineteen of which express a duration which is *certainly* endless. In the remaining three the duration of future punishment is expressed, agreeable to what has been observed above. From this state of the case, is it not easy to determine whether these words, which in all other instances are used to express a duration which is endless, do mean only a temporary, or an endless duration, when they are used with a design to let us know what is the duration of future punishment?

It is said by some, that this word signifies only an *age*; or *ages*, when it is plural. If it be granted that it is sometimes used for an indefinite age; yet, if the adjective *aionios* is always used

Sect. II.

confiſtent and judicious author, ſhould uſe a particular word above ſeventy times in one ſmall volume; and in every inſtance, evidently make uſe of it to expreſs preciſely the ſame thing; ſo that he could not poſſibly mean any thing elſe, or be miſunderſtood, except in five or ſix of them; ſhould we not think ourſelves warranted to fix the ſame meaning to it, in theſe inſtances, unleſs he had given ſufficient intimation, that he then uſed the word in a different ſenſe? There certainly could be no doubt about his meaning in ſuch a caſe: And if any one ſhould inſiſt upon it, that in theſe ſix places he meant no ſuch thing, as he certainly meant in the other, but ſomething very different, and directly contrary; becauſe the word from which this is derived, does not *neceſſarily* mean any ſuch thing, and is ſometimes uſed in a different ſenſe; would he be thought worthy of any regard?

It is further to be obſerved, that this word is not only conſtantly uſed where the duration to be expreſſed is endleſs, which ſhews the force and meaning of it, as has been obſerved; but it is expreſsly oppoſed to a word which ſignifies a temporary duration, to expreſs directly the contrary. 2 Cor. iv. 18. "For the things which are ſeen, are *temporal*; but the things which are not ſeen, are

uſed to expreſs endleſs duration. ; and the ſubſtantive is conſtantly uſed ſo, when it follows the prepoſition *eis*; and, except two inſtances, theſe are the only words uſed to expreſs the duration of future puniſhment: Who can be at a loſs, whether it be endleſs, or not? Beſides, it would make no ſenſe, but the contrary, to tranſlate the word *age* inſtead of *ever*, or *never*. This may be illuſtrated by an inſtance or two. Joh. vi. 58. " This is that bread which came down from heaven: Not as your fathers did eat manna, and are dead: He that eateth of this bread ſhall live *to an age*." x. 28. " And I give unto them eternal life, and they ſhall not periſh *to an age.*" Heb. v. 6. " Thou art a prieſt *to an age*, after the order of Melchiſedec."

are *eternal.*" If this word signified a temporary duration, i. e. a duration which has an end, it could not be opposed to that which signifies such a duration, though ever so long. And if it did not mean an endless duration, it would have no force or sense at all, in this place; but would signify nothing, and might as well be used to express the duration of the things that are seen, as of things that are not seen; and the words might as properly be put thus : For the things which are seen, are eternal ; but the things which are not seen are temporal; if both words signify only a temporal or limited duration.

Thirdly, It is not only expresly said, in holy scripture, that the future punishment of the wicked shall be *everlasting* ; and yet more emphatically, they shall be punished *forever and ever :* But the endless duration of it is yet more strongly asserted, if possible, by negatives, or expresly denying that it shall have any end.

John the Baptist, speaking of Christ, says, Matth. iii: 12. " Whose fan is in his hand, and he will thoroughly purge his floor, and gather his wheat into the garner : But he will burn up the chaff with *unquenchable fire.*" That is, fire that cannot be put out ; there will be no end to its burning.

Our Saviour expresseth this in a yet more pointed and solemn manner, Mark ix. 43, &c. "And if thy hand offend thee, cut it off: It is better for thee to enter into life maimed, than having two hands, to go into hell, *into the fire that never shall be quenched: Where their worm dieth not, and the fire is not quenched.* And if thy foot offend thee, cut it off: For it is better for thee to enter halt into life, than having two feet, to be cast into hell, *into the fire that never shall be quenched: Where their worm dieth not, and the fire is not quenched.* And if thine eye offend thee, pluck it out : It is better for thee to enter into the kingdom of God with one eye,

than

than having two eyes, to be cast into *hell-fire*: *their worm dieth not, and the fire is not quenched.*"

This is a remarkable and singular passage, in our Saviour, full of love and grace, sets himself to men of future punishment, and persuade them, f particular, awful view of it, to avoid and renounc ry thing that will expose them to it. He *dwells* subject, and particularly mentions the hand, the fo the eye; and with relation to each of these descrit punishment that is connected with not partin them, when they offend. And this punishment presented in strong and frightful colours; it is cast into *hell-fire*; and what adds infinitely to the fulness of it, IT SHALL NEVER BE QUENCHED. T nishment never shall have an end. And he express there shall be no end; not once only, but repeats i and over again, and uses negatives *eight* times, i short discourse, with every one of which he assert this punishment will have no end.

Our Saviour does here, doubtless, allude to the of Isaiah, Chap. lxvi. 24. "And they shall go and look upon the carcases of the men that have gressed against me: *For their worms shall not die, shall the fire be quenched.*"

There are two ways in which the bodies of me consumed after they are dead, viz. by being cas a fire and burned; or left to consume away, and be up of worms, which naturally breed in them. the body is soon consumed by the worm, or by t into which it is cast; and the worm of course dies the fire goes out; the endless duration of the punish of the wicked is asserted by saying, The fire, into they are cast, *shall not be quenched*, or go out, and worm never dies. If they who are cast into this pu ment can ever cease to be, or shall be delivered

L

Sect. II.

it, after they have suffered for a time; then it could not be said, Their worm dieth not, and the fire in which they are burned is not quenched, or put out: For the worm and the fire continue, only by the continuance of the subject upon which they prey: When that ceases to be a subject of punishment, the worm dies, and the fire goes out. There could therefore be no other expression, perhaps, thought of, which would with so much precision, and so clearly assert, that the wicked shall be preserved in a state of endless punishment. And this fixes the meaning of Christ's words, when he says, they shall go away into *everlasting punishment, everlasting fire*, if there could otherwise be any possible doubt about it. *Everlasting* fire, the fire in which the wicked shall be tormented *forever and ever*, is, if we will allow Christ himself to tell us, *The fire that never shall be quenched*. *

FOURTHLY,

* They who hold that the wicked will be annihilated, after a temporary punishment, have indeed said, in order to evade the force of this passage, these expressions are so far from asserting the endless duration of the wicked, in a state of punishment, that the contrary is necessarily implied, viz. that they shall soon be destroyed, by ceasing to exist. They say, "There is something absurd and *contradictory* in the image made use of, if we suppose chaff, &c. thrown into an unquenchable fire, and yet not to be consumed and destroyed in that fire; or a living creature cast into it, and yet preserved alive forever in it: For throwing into the fire is always understood to be the most effectual way to *destroy* a thing: And the *less extinguishable* the fire is, the *more certainly* will the subject thrown in be consumed." *Mr. Bourn's letter to Dr. Chandler.*

ANSWER. It is true, that combustible things, which men cast into the fire, are soon consumed: Consequently there is no such thing in this world as unquenchable fire; because whatever is proper fuel for the fire, will be consumed, and burnt up, and the fire will of course be extinguished. And therefore

FOURTHLY, The future punifhment of the wicked is proved to be endlefs, not only by its being exprefsly faid in the fcripture to be *everlafting*, or *eternal*, and that it fhall endure *forever and ever*; and alfo in a pointed manner declared, that it fhall *never end*, as has been fhown: But from many other paffages of fcripture, in which this truth is plainly, and even neceffarily implied. Matth.

therefore cafting chaff, or a dead body, into the fire, would not be a fit emblem of endlefs punifhment, had it not been faid of *this fire*, that it is unquenchable, and never fhall be put out. Were not the punifhment endlefs, there could be no need of faying the fire fhall never be quenched; and it could not be faid with truth: But this fixes the idea, and determines that what is meant by chaff, or whatever is caft into this fire of hell, cannot be confumed by the fire, nor will be taken out of it; but continue without end, to be the fubject for the fire to feed upon, and to prevent its going out. In this view only, there is a perfect confiftence and propriety in thefe expreffions. And to fuppofe the wicked will be wholly deftroyed in this fire, fo as to ceafe to exift, or ever be taken out of it, is to fuppofe it is extinguifhable, and will be actually put out; and therefore to call it *unquenchable* fire, would be indeed " moft abfurd and contradictory " In this view, the manifeft weaknefs and abfurdity of the following confident affertion, appear in a ftriking light. "There is, indeed, fo direct a contradiction between the idea of preferving any creature alive, and that of throwing it into a fire, a fire that cannot be extinguifhed; that if duly confidered, it is amazing how men came to join fo oppofite ideas together, or imagine them to be confiftent." [*Mr. Bourn.*] Do not they, who talk thus greatly err, not underftanding the fcriptures, nor knowing the power of God? There is indeed a direct contradiction between the idea of *their* ceafing to exift, who are caft into the fire. as fuel by which it continues to burn, and that being, at the fame time, fire that cannot be extinguifhed: For the extinction of the fire, and of their exiftence, are neceffarily connected, and indeed one and the fame thing. It is true, that *men* are not able to preferve any creature alive, when they have

Sect. II.

Matth. xxvi. 24. Our Saviour says, The Son of man goeth as it is written of him; but wo unto that man by whom the Son of man is betrayed: *It had been good for*

have cast it into the fire: But GOD is able to preserve a creature in endless punishment, and the most extreme torture; and so to cause the fire of his wrath to be unquenchable, and to burn without end. And if this were not a fact, there could be no such thing as a worm that never dies, or fire that is not quenched. In these words we are expresly told, that there is such a thing; and that GOD, who is able, will do it: And they are not capable of any other consistent sense. Therefore that they should not be taken in this sense, by any man, but in the directly contrary, viz. That the punishment of the wicked *will not* be endless, is indeed amazing!

The advocates for the final salvation of all men, have not been able to give a more satisfactory or consistent sense of this passage, than those just mentioned. It stands as an impregnable bulwark, in defence of endless punishment; which will forever baffle and confound all who dare oppose it. They in the first place say, "This declaration of our Saviour can prove no more than that *the torments of the wicked shall last as long as their next state of existence lasts*, without determining how long that shall be. If their worm prey upon them without ceasing, *as long as they are in hell*, it is to them, strictly and rigidly speaking, a worm that does not die. So if the fire torments them *as long as they exist in the next state*, it is *to them*, a fire which is not quenched, though their existence in that state may not be absolutely eternal." [Salvation for all men, lately printed in Boston. p. 22, 23.]

What has been observed above, sufficiently exposes the weakness and absurdity of all this. According to this interpretation, the worm that lives till the carcase on which it feeds is consumed, or is taken out of its reach, *doth not die*, and *never dies*, though upon this *it dies* infallibly and immediately. And that fire which burns till the fuel which is cast into it is consumed, or taken out of it, which may be before it has burned one minute, and then is immediately extinguished, is a fire *which never shall be extinguished!* At most *for that man, if he had not been born."* Not to be born, is the same as to have no exiſtence: Therefore it is here ſaid of Judas, that his exiſtence was worſe than non-exiſtence: Which could not be true, if he were to be happy moſt, this expoſition makes our Saviour ſay only this, That the future puniſhment of the wicked *ſhall continue as long as it ſhall continue*; and no one can determine from his words, any thing about the duration of it, or whether it ſhall continue one hour! This they call *ſtrict argument*, and *ſtrictly and rigidly ſpeaking*. The reader will judge whether it does not deſerve another name.

But they do not ſeem to be quite ſatiſfied with this comment, and therefore add the following words: "But the moſt *plain, eaſy* and *ſatisfactory* anſwer is—That theſe words are taken from the book of Iſaiah's prophecy, and allude to the puniſhment of thoſe whoſe bodies were either burned in the valley of Hinnom, or permitted to lie on the ground in the form of dead carcaſes, to be fed upon by worms. And conſequently, as the fire which burned theſe bodies, and the worms that fed on them, can in no other ſenſe be ſaid *not to be quenched*, and *not to die*, than this, that they continued till theſe carcaſes were conſumed; ſo may it be ſaid of the worm that preys on the wicked in hell, and of the fire that torments them, that the one dieth not, and the other is not quenched, till they have certainly effected the diſſolution, or death of wicked men, in the future ſtate."

ANSWER. It is granted that *theſe words, Where their worm dieth not, and the fire is not quenched*, are taken from the prophet Iſaiah; and that they allude to the diſſolution of dead bodies, by being eat of worms, or conſumed by fire: But it cannot be granted that, *conſequently*, our Saviour, by theſe words, "Where their worm *dieth not*, and the fire *is not quenched,*" means a worm that *dieth*, and a fire that *is quenched* very ſoon: For this is to ſuppoſe he *means* directly contrary to what he *ſays*. In the valley of Hinnom the worm died and the fire was extinguiſhed, when the dead carcaſes were eaten up by the former, or burned by the latter: But Chriſt ſays, there is no parallel in this reſpect, between theſe, and the worm and fire, in hell: For *there* their worm *doth not die*, and the fire *is not quenched*

happy forever, after suffering a temporary punishment, though ever so long and severe. Judas is therefore, in these words, sentenced to endless punishment. And there is the same reason why *all* impenitent sinners should be punished without end, as that Judas should. ||

Our saviour says, Luk. xii. 10. " Whosoever shall speak a word against the son of man, it shall be forgiven him; but unto him that blasphemeth against the Holy Ghost, *it sha'l not be forgiven.*" And if such an one can never be forgiven, then he cannot be saved ; but must be cursed and punished, as long as he exists. This is

quenched. And the only reason of this is plain, viz. because the subjects on which they prey, which are food for the one, and fuel for the other, never will be consumed, as they are in this world; but continue without end, and the smoke of their torment ascendeth up forever and ever. No advance therefore appears to be made, in this *most plain, easy* and *satisfactory* answer, unless it be in finding out, that our Saviour *means* one thing, and *says* another. Let him to whom this is *plain, easy* and *satisfactory*, avail himself of the advantage.

When they speak of " the *dissolution* and *death* of wicked men, in the future state," who can tell what they mean, unless it be annihilation, or a total cessation of existence ? If one should read only what is said on this text, which has been now quoted, he would naturally conclude they meant this, and held that the punishment of the wicked would end with the end of their existence, they being utterly consumed. But this is contrary to the title of the pamphlet, and most that it contains. What then do they mean by " The *dissolution* and *death* of wicked men, in the future state ?"

The truth of the case seems to be this : The quotation is made from Mr. Scott, or "*one and another*" of his sentiment ; who held that the wicked, after they have been punished for a time, will be wholly consumed, and cease to exist. No wonder therefore, we find an unintelligible jumble and inconsistence, when the advocates for the *salvation of all men*, to support their scheme, quote from those who held directly the contrary. || See note, page 75.

is expressed in different words by St. Mark, Chap, iii. 29. "He that shall blaspheme against the Holy Ghost, hath never forgiveness; but is in danger of eternal damnation." In St. Matth. xii. 31, 32. it is said "The blasphemy against the Holy Ghost *shall not be forgiven unto men*: But whosoever speaketh against the Holy Ghost, it shall not be forgiven him, *neither in this world, neither in the world to come.*"* Here it is asserted by Christ in the strongest terms, that this sin *shall not be forgiven.* Therefore they who are guilty of this sin, must suffer endless punishment, unless they can have eternal life without forgiveness.

What is said, Heb. x. 26, 27. serves to illustrate these words of Christ, "For if we sin wilfully after that we have received the knowledge of the truth, *there remaineth no more sacrifice for sins:* But a certain fearful looking-for of judgment, and fiery indignation, which shall devour the adversaries." Where there is no sacrifice for sin, there cannot be forgiveness of sin: Therefore all who commit this sin, and all who die in their sins, are got beyond forgiveness, as the sacrifice for sin does not extend to them.

That the wicked will never be released from punishment, and pass from hell into the abodes of the blessed, is asserted by our Saviour in the words in which he represents Abraham speaking to the rich man, Luk. xvi. 26. "And besides all this, between us and you there is a great gulf *fixed:* So that they that would pass from hence to you, cannot; *neither can they pass to us, that would come from thence.*"

Agreeable to this is what Christ hath declared since his exaltation, and when he is speaking his *last words* to his church and to the world. Rev. xxii. 10, &c. "And he saith unto me, seal not the sayings of the prophecy of this book: For the time is at hand; he that

* See note, page 76.

that is unjuft, let him be unjuft ftill; and he which is filthy, let him be filthy ftill; and he that is righteous, let him be righteous ftill; and he that is holy, let him be holy ftill. And behold I come quickly; and my reward is with me, to give every man according as his work fhall be."

The time here fpoken of is evidently the time when the events foretold in this book fhall be accomplifhed; when Chrift will come to judgment, and reward every man, according as his work in this life fhall be found to have been, whether good or evil. And then, he fays, every man's character fhall be fixed, and remain forever as it fhall then be found to be. He that is then unjuft, and filthy, fhall ftill continue fo, without any poffibility of being recovered to rectitude and purity, at any future period. And on the other hand, he that is then found righteous and holy, fhall be confirmed in holinefs, and continue fo to all eternity. What could more fully exprefs the fixed ruin, and endlefs punifhment of the wicked! And what words could be invented, more directly againft their notion who dream, that they who fhall appear unrighteous at the day of judgment, fhall in fome after period become holy and enter into everlafting life? If the exalted head of the church here declares, that they who fhall be found righteous at the day of judgment, fhall continue fo forever, without any danger or poffibility of ever falling from their righteoufnefs; which all allow to be fo; how is it poffible for any one not to fee, that he equally, and in the fame ftrong terms declares, that he who fhall then be found unjuft, fhall continue fo from that time, without any poffibility of being recovered to holinefs, even as long as the righteous fhall be righteous ftill?

THERE are many other paffages of fcripture, which are clearly inconfiftent with the falvation of all men;

and

and which, of confequence, neceffarily imply the endlefs punifhment of the wicked. Thefe are too numerous to be particularly mentioned: But they will be pointed out to the reader, who attends to the bible, by being ranked under the following heads.

1. The everlafting life and happinefs of the righteous, and the deftruction and punifhment of the wicked, are, in a multitude of inftances, and commonly, fet in oppofition to each other, as two direct contraries: Which could not be a proper way of reprefenting it, or agreeable

‖ In order to evade the evidence of future, endlefs punifhment from thefe words, it has been faid [See fome deductions from the fyftem promulgated in the pages of divine revelation, p. 21.] It Judas had given up the Ghoft before he had been born, he would have efcaped all the exquifite diftrefs which he fuffered in this life, and fo have been happy ferever, *without being born into this ftate of mifery.* This reprefents Chrift as folemnly pronouncing an awful wo on Judas, which yet was nothing more than that which comes on every man that is born; and is therefore equally true of every man, as of the traitor: For every man is born unto trouble as the fparks fly upward; and his life is *full of trouble.* All which they might have efcaped by not being born. Solomon fays, It is better not to be born, i. e. not to exift, than to have an exiftence in this State only. Is not this to make our Saviour fay nothing; or rather to trifle about the moft folemn matters?

Not to be born is oppofed to exiftence; and the only natural meaning of the phrafe is, not to come into exiftence.

It is further faid, that Chrift promifed Judas, that he, with the other difciples, fhould fit on *twelve* thrones, judging the twelve tribes of Ifrael; which is inconfiftent with his being miferable forever.

Anfwer. We are told in the firft chapter of the Acts of the Apoftles, that this was not true of Judas perfonally; but of the *twelve* when their number was filled up, by chufing one to take the place of Judas, from which he fell by his tranfgreffion, able to the truth, if they were both to enjoy everlasting life together, in the kingdom of God. If the wicked are to be afflicted but for a time, and then delivered from misery, and be as greatly happy as the righteous and as long; then their perishing, their punishment, is as light as nothing, and but for a moment, compared with the eternal weight of glory and happiness, which they shall enjoy equally with the righteous; and therefore cannot be set in opposition to eternal life, or the blessedness of the righteous, as this would be highly improper, and a gross misrepresentation. A few instances, out of many which might be mentioned, will be sufficient to illustrate this remark. Psal. xxxvii. 18,

* Some have said this last expression means no more than that this sin should not be forgiven, under the Jewish or Christian dispensation, as the word here translated *world* is used sometimes for *an age*: And *this world* may signify the Mosaic dispensation, and *the world to come* the Christian, and not the future state.

Answer. It is said in the preceeding verse, and in the other Evangelists, that this sin *shall not be forgiven unto men*, without any limitation or exception whatever: And these words that are here added, *neither in this world, neither in the world to come*, cannot be considered as limiting the other words, as they are not in the other Evangelists: But they are added to express the same thing in a yet more strong and striking manner. We know what our Saviour meant by *the world to come*, by his use of it elsewhere, Mark. x. 38. "There is no man that hath left house, or brethren, &c. for my sake and the gospel's, but he shall receive an hundred fold now in this time, *and in the world to come eternal life*." Here the world to come means the future state, and an endless or eternal state, if the followers of Christ will be happy without end.

"It is clearly shown by Dr. Whitby, that this was used as a *proverbial expression*, and that it only signified, *a thing should never be*, when it was said, It *shall not be, either in this world, or the world to come*. Dr. Doddridge on Matth. xii, 32.

18, 20. "The Lord knoweth the days of the upright; and their inheritance shall be forever. But the wicked shall perish." &c. Here the perishing of the wicked is opposed to the everlasting, incorruptible inheritance of the righteous; which could not be, if their perishing were consistent with their enjoying this everlasting inheritance, as well and as long as the righteous: For, on that supposition, it is as true of the wicked, as of the upright, that their inheritance shall be forever; and, in this respect, there is no distinction, much less opposition. Therefore, to set them in opposition would be a misrepresentation, and not agreeable to the truth. If the perishing of the wicked runs parallel with the inheritance of the upright, and forever excludes them from this inheritance; then these words express a great and important truth; but on any other supposition, they are perfectly unintelligible, or not true.

These same remarks will apply to those words of Christ and John the Baptist. Joh. iii. 15, &c. "That whosoever believeth in him, *should not perish*, but have eternal life. For God so loved the world that he gave his only begotten son, that whosoever believeth in him, *should not perish*, but have everlasting life." Here it is implicitly asserted that he who does not believe in Christ shall *perish*; but if *to perish*, is not to be exluded from eternal life, with what propriety or truth can this be set in opposition to having eternal life, when it is as true of the unbeliever, as of the believer, that he shall have eternal life; and this happy lot is as much the portion of the former, as of the latter? "He that believeth in the son, *hath everlasting life*; and he that believeth not the son, shall not see life; but the wrath of God abideth on him." Here what is necessarily implied in our Saviour's words, just mentioned, is expressed and we are told what is meant by the unbelievers perishing, perish'ng, *He shall not see life*; but the wrath of God abideth on him, as long as he is excluded from life, and that must be as long as the believer enjoys everlasting life.

Rom. ii. 6, &c: "Who will render to every man according to his deeds. To them who by patient continuance in well doing, seek for glory, and honor, and immortality, *eternal life*; but to them that are contentious, and do not obey the truth, but obey unrighteousness, indignation and wrath, tribulation and anguish, upon every soul that doth evil." Here the rewards or portions of the righteous and of the wicked are contrasted, and opposed to each other: But if the latter shall have glory, honor, peace, and eternal life, as well as the former; why are the former represented as distinguished from the latter in *this*, which is common to them both? 2 Thess. ii. 10. &c. "And for this cause God shall send them strong delusion, that they should believe a lie, that they all might *be damned*, &c. But we are bound always to give thanks to God for you, brethren, beloved of the Lord, because God hath from the beginning chosen you *to salvation*." Here salvation and damnation are opposed; and christians are distinguished from those who believe a lie, and obey unrighteousness to their own damnation, and set in opposition to them, as being *chosen to salvation*. But if salvation and damnation are so consistent with each other, that all who are damned shall be the subjects of eternal salvation, and are *chosen to salvation*, as really as the true christian, what does the Apostle mean by all this?

Jam. iv. 12. "There is one lawgiver who is able to *save*, and to *destroy*."— Salvation and destruction are here opposed, as inconsistent with each other; which could not be, if there were no destruction inconsistent with eternal salvation.

Matth. vii. 13, 14. "Enter ye in at the strait gate;

for wide is the gate and broad is the way that leadeth to deftruction. Becaufe ftrait is the gate and narrow is the way that leadeth unto life."

If all the wicked who go in the broad way, do enter in to life as certainly, and nearly as foon, as they who walk in the narrow way; only the former pafs through a little more fevere difcipline than the other; is not the broad way as certain a road to life as the other? How then can life and deftruction, and thefe different roads, be oppofed to each other?

2. The holy fcriptures every where reprefent the fervants of God, who fear and truft in him, as happy and bleffed: And on the other hand, fpeak of thofe who go on in evil ways through this life, as moft miferable, and pronounces woes and curfes on them; which is not confiftent with their being alike happy forever in the kingdom of Chrift. To the former innumerable promifes are made, that no evil fhall come near them; that all things fhall work for their good, and promote their beft intereft; and that they fhall have eternal life: To the latter no good is promifed, and nothing but evil is fpoken and foretold of them; for which there could be no reafon, if endlefs happinefs awaited the latter, as certainly as the former. If this were the cafe, they would both be bleffed; and there would be no fuch great difference between them. Though the wicked fhall fuffer for a time; yet, if this fhall iffue in their eternal happinefs, and be the fpecial and neceffary mean of it too, what St. Paul fays of chriftians may, with truth and propriety, be applied to *them*: That their fufferings, for a time, are not worthy to be compared with the glory which fhall be revealed in them: And their light affliction, which is but for a moment, compared with endlefs happinefs, worketh for them a far more exceeding and eternal weight of glory. And St: Peter's

Peter's prayer for suffering christians will be answered for all that are in hell, or ever shall be there; and may with as great propriety be made for them. "The God of all grace, who hath called us into his eternal glory by Jesus Christ, *after that ye have suffered a while, make you perfect,*" &c. And the words of Christ to his disciples, may be applied to them. In all your sufferings, "Rejoice, and be exceeding glad; for great is your reward in heaven." Why then is God's word so full of threatnings of evil to the wicked, without the least intimation of any good coming to them; and of promises of nothing but good to the righteous? Why does God say to the righteous, that it shall be well with him, for they shall eat of the fruit of their doings. Wo unto the wicked, it shall be ill with him; for the reward of his hands shall be given him. There is no peace, saith the Lord, unto the wicked; while he speaks peace, and nothing but peace, unto his people, and to his saints. Psal. lxxxv. 8.———Prov. xii. 21. "There shall no evil happen to the just; but the wicked shall be filled with mischief." The just suffer much evil; but it is no evil to them, because it is designed for their best good, and will issue in it. And if the future sufferings of the wicked are temporary, and designed to purge them from their sins; are necessary in order to this, and will have this happy effect; why is it not as true of them, that no evil shall happen to them? Why are they, with respect to this, set in opposition to the just, and marked out for nothing but mischief and evil? Prov. xiii. 21. "Evil pursueth sinners: But to the righteous good shall be repaid." Psal. xxxiv. 19, &c. "Many are the afflictions of the righteous: But the Lord delivereth him out of them all. Evil shall slay the wicked; and they that hate the righteous shall be desolate." If the sufferings of the wicked in hell are in mercy to them, and defigned to bring them to repentance, and they fhall be delivered out of them all; then, what is here faid of the righteous is juſt as true of the wicked; though their afflictions and fufferings may be many, yet the Lord will deliver them out of them all. Why then is directly the oppofite faid of the wicked, that *evil fhall flay or dſtroy* him; when all the evil that comes upon him will work for his good, and his deliverance is certain and haftening? Pſal. xciii. 12, 13. " Bleffed is the man whom thou chafteneſt, O Lord, and teacheſt him out of thy law; that thou mayeſt give him reſt from the days of adverfity, until the pit be digged for the wicked." If the future puniſhment of the wicked be of the nature of correction, and God is hereby chaftening him, that he may teach him wifdom, and bring him to his duty, that he may be delivered from all adverfity and evil; and this ſhall be the happy confequence; may he not with as much reafon and propriety be pronounced bleffed, as the righteous? Why then is he always curfed, and fet in oppofition to the righteous, in this refpect?

If the wicked fhall certainly be delivered from hell, as foon as he repents, and makes his fubmiffion to God, and God inflicts this evil on him, with a defign to bring him to this; then what is faid of the children of God is as true of the wicked in hell, That God chafteneth them *for their profit, that they might be partakers of his holinefs.* And if this be true, are they not *bleffed?* The whole current of fcripture, on this head, is perfectly inconfiftent with the temporary puniſhment of the wicked, and their eternal falvation: And therefore evidently afferts their endlefs deftruction,

3. The fcripture reprefents the wicked, when rejected and caſt into hell, as repenting and earneſtly defiring

firing and seeking deliverance; but all in vain; for their repentance and cries will not be regarded: Which is inconsistent with their punishment being of the nature of merciful chastisement, in order to their obtaining eternal life, which shall be granted whenever they submit, and ask deliverence: Yea, strongly imports that they never shall be heard and delivered.

Prov. i. 24, &c. "Because I have called, and ye refused, &c. I also will laugh at your calamity and mock when your fear cometh; when distress and anguish cometh upon you. *Then shall they call upon me, but I will not answer; they shall seek me early, but they shall not find me.*" Matth. xxv. 11, 12. "Afterwards came also the other virgins, saying, *Lord, Lord, open unto us*: But he answered and said, Verily I say unto you, *I know you not.*" Luk. xiii. 24, &c. "Strive to enter in at the strait gate: For many, I say unto you, *will seek to enter in, and shall not be able.* When once the master of the house is risen up, and hath shut to the door; and ye begin to stand without, *and to knock at the door, saying, Lord, Lord, upon unto us*: And he shall answer, and say unto you, I know you not whence ye are: *Depart from me, all ye workers of iniquity*: There shall be weeping and gnashing of teeth, when ye shall see Abraham, and Isaac and Jacob, and all the prophets in the kingdom of God, and you yourselves *thrust out.*" According to this, when the door of mercy is once shut, it will be shut forever; and however earnestly they who are excluded may desire and seek admittance, it will be all in vain. *

Christ

---

* These words of Christ are in consequence of a question which was asked by one, in the following words: "Lord, are there few that shall be saved? If our Lord knew that *all* should be saved, and that this was a joyful, glorious doctrine,

Christ represents the rich man in hell as earnestly praying for a little mitigation of his torment; but meeting with a denial: And Abraham tells him, There is a great gulf *fixed*, so that they *who would come out of hell cannot*. No desires of deliverance that will ever take place in hell, can avail, or be regarded. In the epistle to the Hebrews, the case of those who come short of being real christians in this world, and so are cast into hell, is represented by Esau, who, by selling his birth right, lost it forever. "For ye know how that *afterward, when he would have inherited the blessing, he was rejected: For he found no place of repentance, though he sought it carefully with tears.*" This representation must be very contrary to truth, if any repentance and cries for mercy, that shall take place in hell, will be regarded, and obtain deliverance; which will be the case if they are ever delivered. All these passages of scripture, therefore, and others of the like tenor, are opposed to the deliverance of the wicked from hell, by their being brought to repentance, and to cry for mercy; and are not consistent with any future punishment, except an endless one. And this representation militates directly against the notion that future punishment is salutary, and inflicted by God in mercy to the wicked,

trine, necessary to be preached in order to set the character of God in the best light, and make the brightest display of divine grace; and was perfectly suited to turn men from sin, and lead them to embrace the gospel, and excite in them the highest gratitude, joy and praise; why did he neglect such a good opportunity to declare this very important, useful truth? Why did he not only wholly conceal it; but make a contrary representation, teaching that all who did neglect salvation in this life, would be shut out of the kingdom of heaven, and cast into hell; and that no repentance, earnest seeking and intreaties, for deliverance, will then be to any purpose? Can these questions be answered?

wicked, and tending to their repentance and amendment, in order to their being fitted for eternal happiness. Directly the reverse of this is the idea held up in these passages, and, indeed, throughout the whole bible. The door of mercy is shut. God punishes them in anger, to show his wrath, and make his power known. He will not regard their repentance, nor hear their cries for mercy; but will laugh at their calamity, and mock when their destruction falls upon them: And they will be abandoned to perfect despair and endless wo!

The evidence contained in the scripture, of the future and *endless* punishment of the wicked, is now laid before the reader. And is it not as clearly revealed, that this punishment will never end, as any truth whatever, which is contained in the bible? It is, at least, as certain, from divine revelation, that this punishment will be endless, as that the happiness of the righteous will be so. Yea, it cannot be conceived how the eternal duration of the punishment of the wicked could be more plainly and fully expressed. Language does not afford words more expressive of this, than those which are used; and they are used in such a manner and connexion as to fix their meaning as clearly, and as much beyond all doubt, as is possible: And this is expressed, or necessarily implied, so often, and in so many different ways, that there is a multiplicity of evidence, and demonstration rises on demonstration; so that, if the doctrine of endless punishment be not most clearly revealed, it is doubtless impossible it should be made known, by any words, or in any way whatsoever.

This will well account for the general belief of this doctrine, in the christian world, from the days of the apostles, down to this time: And though there have been some individuals in almost every age, who

who have renounced it, and have attempted to perſuade others to reject it: Yet comparatively few, who have paid any regard to the bible, have hearkened to them. And if the diſbelief of endleſs puniſhment, and even of any future puniſhment at all, ſhould now prevail, and have a wider ſpread than ever before, it will be doubtleſs owing to a greater and more general prevalence of blinding moral corruption, and the greater power of Satan, which it is foretold he ſhall have in the world, previous to the flouriſhing of the kingdom of Chriſt: * Which will produce a remakable degree of infatuation and error, even *ſtrong deluſion*, in believing that firſt and moſt pernicious L I E, which the great deceiver told in this world, and has been ever ſince endeavouring to propagate, YE SHALL NOT SURELY DIE. And it may be juſtly expected, that the propagation of this deluſion, will promote a total diſregard to divine revelation.

SECTION III.

CONTAINING an Examination of thoſe Paſſages of Scripture, which the Oppoſers of the Doctrine of endleſs Puniſhment, and Advocates for the Salvation of all Men, have thought to be favourable to their Cauſe.

THESE ſcriptures muſt be full and expreſs, and moſt evidently oppoſite to the doctrine of endleſs puniſhment;

* Rev. xvi. 13, 14. And I ſaw three unclean ſpirits, like frogs, come out of the mouth of the dragon, and out of the mouth of the beaſt, and out of the mouth of the falſe prophet. For they are the *ſpirits of the devils*, working miracles, which go forth unto the kings of the earth, and of the whole world, &c."

ment; and so worded, & in such connexion, as not to be capable of a construction consistent with it, in order to have any weight in the mind of an honest inquirer, who has attended to the scriptures which have been produced; wherein it is so often, so expressly, and in so many ways asserted. And if any such passages are to be found, which can by no means, in a fair and honest way, be reconciled to the future and endless punishment of the wicked; an insuperable difficulty will be introduced, viz. That the bible is inconsistent with itself, so that one part cannot be reconciled with another!

It is not uncommon, for men to appeal to the scriptures, in order to support the grossest errors, and think they find much in the bible in their favor. Therefore, in the matter before us, it becomes us carefully to examine those scriptures, which are produced as inconsistent with endless punishment; and whatever plausible gloss has been put upon them, if they appear capable of a natural, fair construction, perfectly consistent with it, we shall have the satisfaction of seeing the consistency and harmony of the holy scriptures on this point; and this doctrine will, if possible, be more confirmed.

It would be needless, if it were practicable, to consider *every text*, which has been mentioned by those who plead for universal salvation, as favouring their cause. It will be sufficient to attend to those upon which they appear to have the most dependence: And if it can be proved those are nothing to their purpose, the rest will, of course, be given up. To prove that all men will be saved, those passages of scripture are produced, which speak of the sufficiency, and designed extent of the atonement; made by Christ, for the sins of men; such are the following. John i. 29. " Behold the Lamb of God, which

which taketh away the *fin of the world*." 1 Tim. ii. 6. "Who gave himself a ransom *for all.*" Heb. ii. 9." That he, by the grace of God, should taste death for *every man.*" 1 Joh ii. 2. "And he is the propitiation for our fins: And not for ours only, but also for the fins *of the whole world.*"

In order to see the true import of these scripture passages, and a number of others, which are to be mentioned, the following observations must be made, and kept in view.

1. The atonement which Christ has made for the fins of men, by his obedience unto death, is every way sufficient for the salvation of all men; as sufficient for all, as for any one. This has effectually removed the difficulty, the bar which was in the way of the salvation of any one of mankind; and this is as fully removed with respect to all, as to one; and there is nothing of that kind, which Christ came to remove out of the way, by his atonement, in the way of the salvation of the whole world. Had it not been for this atonement, the fins of men had barred the way of their salvation, and mercy could not have been extended to them. Christ, by making atonement for sin, has taken this obstacle out of the way of man's salvation, even the salvation of *all men*, of the *whole world*. It is in this sense, that he has "finished the transgression, and made an end of sin."* · In this sense, he has taken away the sin of the world; is the propitiation for the fins of the whole world; and has "*Put away fin*, by the sacrifice of himself." ‖ This observation alone, opens an easy, plain, natural, and important meaning to the passages now under consideration, and to others which will be mentioned; a meaning which has no immediate respect to the

actual

---

* Dan. ix. 24. ‖ Heb. ix. 26.

actual salvation of all men; and is perfectly consistent with those numerous declarations in sacred writ, that multitudes shall, notwithstanding, perish forever. Though sin is, in this true, important sense, taken wholly out of the way of the salvation of all men; yet something further is necessary, in order to their actual salvation; which must take place, or they will die in their sins, and perish forever. And what this is, we find clearly stated, and abundantly declared, by Christ himself, and his apostles. Our Saviour has fixed it, beyond all dispute; Joh. iii. 16. "For God so loved *the world*, that he gave his only begotten Son, *that whosoever believeth on him*, should not perish, but have everlasting life." The Saviour is given to the world: And he has taken away the sin of the world, by the sacrifice of himself; nevertheless, they only who believe on him, shall be saved; and they who refuse and reject him, shall perish; for "He that *believeth not* shall be damned." What can be plainer than all this? And how can the scriptures be consistent, if this interpretation be not admitted?

2. It follows from the preceding observations, that the salvation procured for man, by the atonement of Christ, and opened in the gospel, is a *common salvation*. There is sufficient provision made for the salvation of all. It is therefore *for all*, proposed and offered *to all*, without distinction: It is offered to their acceptance, that whosoever *is willing*, and does accept of it, shall be saved, and none can fail of this salvation, but by a continued neglect and obstinate rejection of it, to the end of life. This salvation, therefore, *belongs to all*, in this sense: It is salvation for all men, the whole world, if they will accept of it, or unless they reject it. It comes to one as well as another, without distinction. This appears, and is expressed, in the orders Christ gave to his disciples;

pels; and in them, to all who are authorized to preach the gospel. " Go teach *all nations*. Go ye *into all the world,* and preach the gospel *to every creature*." That is, to *all men*. " He that believeth and is baptized, shall be saved; but he that believeth not, shall be damned." If the declared *will* and command of Christ had been properly regarded and executed; and were it not for the inexcusable wickedness of men, in opposing or neglecting the gospel and the great salvation it proclaims, and offers to all, every son and daughter of Adam, on earth, would soon have heard this good news, and would have believed unto salvation; and every one of mankind, who have lived from that day to this, would have been saved, having come to the knowledge of the truth.

This gives a clear and determinate sense to the words of St. Paul, 1 Tim. ii. 1, &c. " I exhort therefore, that first of all supplications, prayers, intercessions, and giving of thanks be made for *all men*. For this is good and acceptable in the sight of God our Saviour; *who will have all men to be saved*, and come to the knowledge of the truth." The apostle knew that it was the *express will* and command of our Saviour, who is God, that the gospel should be preached to *all men*, that they might come to the knowledge of the truth, and be saved; unless they should wickedly reject it, when offered to them. And how could this be expressed better, or in more proper and intelligible language, than in the words just quoted? And if this be the most natural, easy, and consistent sense of the words, then they are perfectly consistent with the eternal destruction of all who, in this life, reject the gospel, or neglect this great salvation. *

The

---

* To make out from this passage, that *all men* will be actually saved, it has been asserted, that " G*o*d *authoritatively wills*

Sect. III.

The propriety and importance of such expressions as are now under consideration, will further appear by observing:

3dly.

wills the salvation of all: Wills it as a being of supreme, uncontroulable power, a being that *will* be obeyed in spite of the corrupt dispositions of men, &c." But this is said without any proof; yea, contrary to the clearest evidence. God our Saviour *willed* and commanded that the gospel should be preached to every creature: So that the whole world might be saved, unless they should perseveringly reject the salvation offered: But this *his will* has been opposed by men, so that it has not taken effect, and millions have perished by this neglect. And this is the *will* spoken of in the text under consideration. Besides, if this meant the *efficacious will* of God our Saviour, a will with which the event is necessarily connected, why has it not taken place in this world?

God can as easily bring all to the knowledge of the truth and to a state of salvation in this life, as in any future time: Why then does he not effect it here; but put it off to a distant period, in the unseen world; with respect to which not a word is said of bringing men to the knowledge of the truth, and to salvation, who die in their sins? Or rather, why will any *imagine* this, when there is not a tittle in this passage to support it, but all is against it?

God our Saviour has provided salvation for all men; has formed an institution, which comprehends, and will infallibly effect the salvation of all men, if properly regarded and improved by men; and this he hath willed and commanded to be done. It is his express will and command, that this gospel be preached to *every creature*, to *all men*, and he *wills* and commands *all men* every where, upon hearing this gospel, to repent and believe the gospel, unto salvation. In this sense he wills that all men should be saved: But this his will has been resisted by the folly and obstinacy of men; as it was in another instance, of which he himself speaks. Matth. xxiii. 37. "O Jerusalem, Jerusalem, thou that killest the prophets, and stonest them which are sent unto thee, *how often* WOULD *I have gathered thy children together*, even as a hen gathereth

her

Sect. III.

3dly. The Jews had very contracted, unworthy notions of God's defigns of mercy to men, and of the work and falvation of the Meffiah. They confined this falvation wholly to themfelves, and confiderd all other nations as outcafts, wholly excluded from God's favor, and all benefits in the kingdom of Chrift; unlefs they became Jews by circumifion. This was a fixed and favourite doctrine among the Jews; and it was not eafy for them to give it wholly up, and free themfelves from all the influence of it, when they embraced chriftianity. The apoftles themfelves, for fometime after the refurrection of Chrift, formed their notions of falvation by this Jewifh prejudice, in which they were educated; and had no thought of offering falvation to the uncircumcifed Gentiles. Several miracles were at length wrought, in order to convince them, that *in every nation* he that feared God, and embraced the gofpel, was accepted of him, and faved, and that God had alfo to the *Gentiles* granted repentance unto life, as well as unto Jews.

And this prejudice remained on the minds of the Jewifh

her chickens under her wings, *and ye* WOULD NOT !" Here is the fame word in the original as in the text under confideration, tranflated *will*, and in this paffage, *would*, and might have been rendered, how often *have I willed* to gather thy children, &c. Here he reprefents himfelf as *willing* the falvation of the inhabitants of Jerufalem; which they prevented taking effect, by their refufal to accept his offered kindnefs. He had made full provifion for their falvation, and had offered to beftow it on them; fo that, had they confented, and accepted the offer, they would have been faved; and this he calls his *willing* to protect and fave them: But notwithftanding this, they perifhed, becaufe *they would not* comply with his kind offer.

But more than enough has been faid to fhew how far the words under confideration are from affording the leaft evidence of the actual falvation of all men.

Sect. III.

Jewish christians for a long time; which the apostle Paul, who was the apostle of the Gentiles, took special care and pains in his epistles, to oppose and eradicate, by asserting, that salvation by Christ was as free, and as much for one nation, as another; and therefore to be preached and offer'd to all nations, and every man, without distinction. And with this view, the expressions under consideration are evidently used, as well as *many others of the like kind*, in the New-testament: And their full meaning, design and importance will not appear, without keeping this in view. This observation may be *illustrated* by reviewing the passage that has been considerd, 1 Tim. ii 1. &c. The true meaning may be expressed in the following paraphrase. " I exhort that christians pray for *all men*, Gentiles as well as Jews, without making any distinction. For this is certainly acceptable to God our Saviour ; who is the God and Saviour, not only of the Jews, but of the Gentiles also ; and has provided salvation equally for all nations, and all men; and has willed and commanded, that the gospel should be preached to all nations, and salvation freely offered to all, without distinction; that they may come to the knowledge of the truth and be saved, unless they perish by their own fault. For there is but one God, who is the God of the Gentiles, as well as of the Jews ; and one Mediator between God and man, even all men, the man Christ Jesus ; whose mediation and atonement therefore does not respect one nation only ; but is unlimited and universal ; and he gave himself a ransom for all, that his gospel might be preached, and salvation offered to all men ; which he determined should be testified and made known in due time ; however ignorant of it, both Jews and Gentiles have been, in ages past. This has indeed been a mystery, which was kept secret since the world began; but now is made manifest,

manifest, and by the scriptures of the prophets, according to the commandment of the everlasting God, *made known to all nations for the obedience of faith*; that is, that " Whosoever believeth may be saved."

The following passages of scripture have been also urged against the doctrine of endless punishment. Gen. iii. 15. " It shall bruise thy head, and thou shalt bruise his heel." 1 Joh iii. 8. "For this purpose the Son of God was manifested, *that he might destroy the works of the devil.*" 1 Cor. xv. 25. " For he must reign, till he hath put all his enemies under his feet." It is said, these scriptures are inconsistent with the continuance of sin and misery forever; for these are among the enemies, which shall be put under the feet of Christ; and are the works of the devil, which he came to destroy. That Satan's head can't be bruised effectually, and his works destroyed, if any of the human race are left in his hands, and finally destroyed in endless sin and misery.

That these declarations do not afford the least ground for such a consequence, will be very evident, by attending to the following observations.

1. The natural and common meaning of a person's having his enemies put under his feet, is his completely defeating and overcoming, and triumphing over them. This was represented by the captains of the men of war in Joshua's army *putting their feet on the necks* of the kings of Canaan. Josh x. 24. This does not imply that the enemies are reconciled to the conqueror, and do cordially submit, and become his friends, and applaud, and rejoice in his conquests; but supposes the contrary, viz. That they continue his enemies, though completely overcome; and they are held under his feet, to answer his ends, and grace his conquest and triumph.

2.

2. The devil will be most effectually subdued; his works will be destroyed, and his head bruised, in the highest sense and degree, when he shall be perfectly defeated and disappointed in all his ends and designs; and every thing he has attempted and done against Christ and his interest, shall be turned against himself, to answer those ends which he constantly sought to defeat by all his attempts; and Christ shall be more honored, and his kingdom more happy and glorious forever, than it could have been, if Satan had never opposed him, or seduced and destroyed any of mankind. This does, not imply that the devil shall ever become a friend to Christ or cease to exist, or that all the human race shall be saved; but the contrary may be necessary, in order to effect this to the highest degree; viz. that the devil and his angels, with all his impenitent followers in this world, be doomed to everlasting punishment, as Christ himself says they shall. And that this is necessary in order to destroy the kingdom and works of the devil most effectually, and to answer the most important ends to Christ and his eternal kingdom, will, it is hoped, be made to appear in the sequel. In this view, these passages of scripture are so far from being inconsistent with endless punishment, that this is necessarily supposed and implied in what they assert.

Another passage of scripture, which refers to the same event, is found in Phil. ii. 10, 11. " That at the name of Jesus every knee should bow, of things in heaven, and things in earth, and things under the earth; and that every tongue should confess, that Jesus Christ is Lord, to the glory of God the Father." This text has been produced as inconsistent with endless punishment, and as a full proof, that all men and devils will be finally saved. The whole weight of their argument, from this passage, lies in the meaning they affix to *bow-*

ing

ing the knee at the name of Christ, and *confessing that Jesus Christ is Lord*. They say, this means a voluntary homage paid to him, as his friends and obedient servants. But what evidence is there of this? The words are as capable of another meaning, as of this, and perfectly agreeable to the design of the apostle here; which is to shew how Christ is exalted and honored, and is to reign until all creatures and things in the universe shall be made subject to him, and his enemies put under his feet. His friends will bow the knee to him, and cheerfully give him the glory due to his name, and joyfully submit to him, and own him as their Lord, and the Lord of all. His enemies also will be obliged to submit to him, and own his power and dominion, and that they are justly condemned and punished by him: And while in punishing them, he will *tread the winepress of the fierceness of the wrath of Almighty God*, it will be to the glory of God the Father. In this sense, this same apostle quotes and uses these words, in his epistle to the Romans, Chap. xiv. 10, &c. "For *we shall all stand before the judgment seat of Christ*. For it is written, As I live, saith the Lord, every knee shall bow to me, and every tongue shall confess to God. So then, every one of us *shall give account of himself to God*." Here the apostle uses the words only to signify, that all shall give an account to Christ as their judge, and consequently receive a sentence according as their works have been, whether good or evil; which he will cause to be properly executed. And may we not, rather *must we not*, understand them in much the same sense, when he uses the same words in another epistle?

The apostle Peter, speaking of Christ, says, Acts iii. 21. "Whom the heavens must receive, until the times of the *restitution of all things*, which God hath spoken by the mouth of all his holy prophets, since the world began."

began." Some have thought these words signify, that all creatures shall be restored to holiness and happiness by Christ. That they import no such thing, will be evident, if the following things be observed.

1. *The restitution of all things* seems to mean nothing else here, but the *accomplishment* of all things which God hath spoken by the mouth of all his holy prophets. This sense is given to the original word, in some translations; and is natural and easy, and agreeable to the following words, which have been cited.

2. *All things* will not be restored to their former state at Christ's second coming, and therefore this cannot be the meaning. This earth and the visible heavens, are reserved unto fire, against the day of judgment, and perdition of ungodly men; when the heavens *shall pass away* with a great noise, and the elements shall *melt with fervent heat*; the earth also and the works that are therein *shall be burnt up*.

3. The time of the restitution of all things, of which the apostle speaks, is the time of Christ's coming to judgment, which is elsewhere called his coming the second time: For the heavens must receive him, till this time of restitution, which they will not do, any longer than to the day of judgment; for then he will "So come in like manner as his disciples saw him go into heaven." Therefore, they who allow there will be any punishment of men and devils after the day of judgment, as all must who will pay any regard to the bible, cannot make this text mean the restoring all creatures to holiness or happiness, consistent with their own notion of the final restitution.

4. If the restitution of all things does not mean only the fulfilment of all the great things which the prophets have foretold, which has been observed as the most natural sense, and will certainly take place at the day of
judgment;

judgment: And if something more, or different, be signified by this expression, it must mean the restitution of all things from the state of disorder and confusion, into which they are fallen by sin, into a state of order, at the day of judgment; when all shall be called to an account, and rebellion shall be silenced and come to a proper issue, and every one be rewarded according to his works; and all obstinate sinners, both men and devils, receive their proper doom and punishment; while the righteous are separated from them, to inherit the kingdom prepared for them: And Christ and his kingdom receive all the advantage of the rebellion that has taken place, and of the endless punishment of the wicked: So that there shall be unspeakably more glory and happiness in the kingdom of God, in consequence of sin, and the endless punishment of the wicked, than could have been without it. When things shall be brought to this state and issue, which certainly they will be at the day of judgment, the *restitution of all things* will take place to the highest degree. Every thing will be set perfectly right; the wicked will receive their proper punishment; all the reproach cast on God's law, government and character will be wiped off, and he shall have his full revenue of glory, by all the sin and punishment of the wicked. Christ shall receive the full reward of his work, and his kingdom have all the advantage of the whole. Who can imagine a more perfect and glorious restitution of all things, than this? *

Another

* Christ says, Matth. xvii. 11, "Elias truly shall first come, and *restore* all things." The same word is used here, as in Act. iii. 21. There it is a substantive, and here a verb; and must signify to regulate, and *reduce things to order*. This the Baptist did, by preaching repentance and reformation, and declaring, that all who refused to comply, should be punished in *unquenchable fire*. Christ will restore all things, by seeing this most completely executed.

Sect. III.

Another text, which is produced in favor of universal salvation, and to oppose the doctrine of endless punishment, is Rom. v. 18. " Therefore, as by the offence of one, judgment came upon all men to condemnation: Even so, by the righteousness of one, the free gift came upon all men, unto justification of life."

Answer. The apostle had particularly stated the way, by which men become interested in the righteousness and salvation exhibited and offered freely to all in the gospel; and proved that this is by faith, or believing in Christ, or receiving him, and the abounding grace, and gift of righteousness by him. And had abundantly insisted, that there is no other possible way for men to have any share in this righteousness and justification by Christ, but by faith. He had mentioned this *above twenty times*, in this epistle, before he comes to these words now under consideration, keeping it constantly in view. It will suffice to cite only three or four instances now, out of more than twenty. Chap. i. 16. " For I am not ashamed of the gospel of Christ, for it is the power of God unto salvation, *to every one that believeth.*" Ch. iii. 22. " Even the righteousness of God, which is by faith of Jesus Christ, *unto all, and upon all them that believe.*" And this chapter begins with the following words, " Therefore, *being justified by faith*, we have peace with God, through our Lord Jesus Christ." And in the sentence immediately preceding the words we are upon, the same thing is brought into view, though the word *faith*, or *believing* is not used. v. 17. " For if by one man's offence, death reigned by one ; much more they which *receive* abundance of grace, and of the gift of righteousness, shall reign in life by one, Jesus Christ." Here the word *receive* is active, and expresses that particular exercise or act, by which men embrace the gospel, or receive Christ; and is the same thing with

Sect. III.

with faith, or believing on Chrift. Joh. i. 12. "But as many as *received* him, to them gave he power to become the fons of God; even to them that *believe on his name.*" He here limits the abundant grace, and gift of righteoufnefs, by which men reign in life, to thofe who *receive* it, or believe on Chrift. For it is in and upon *all them* that *believe.* There was, therefore, no need of repeating this limitation, in the words under confideration, and faying, "Even fo, by the righteoufnefs of one, the free gift came [or comes] upon all men [*who believe*] unto juftification of life." For this is naturally and even *neceffarily* underftood. And it would be doing violence to the words to leave out this idea, and make the apoftle fay, in direct contradiction to what he had fo often afferted before, and laboured to prove; that juftification and falvation comes alike upon all men, believers, and unbelievers, or whether they believe or not. And this not only makes him contradict himfelf, but the exprefs words of Chrift, and John the Baptift, "He that believeth not is condemned already. He that believeth not fhall be damned. He that believeth not the Son, *fhall not fee life*; but the wrath of God *abideth* on him."

The free gift does indeed come to all men, in the offer of the gofpel; and it is wholly owing to the wickednefs of men, difpofing them to flight and reject this falvation, thus brought and coming to them, that all men, even every one of the human race, are not actually faved: But ftill it remains true, that they only who believe, and thankfully *receive* this offered grace and gift of righteoufnefs, fhall be actually juftified, and reign in life by Jefus Chrift: For he that believeth not, after all, fhall be damned.

It has been alfo imagined, that the falvation of all men, is afferted in the viii. Chap. of this Epiftle v. 19.

Sect. III.

v. 19,——23. "For the earnest expectation of the creature waiteth for the manifestation of the sons of God. For the creature was made subject to vanity, not willingly, but by reason of him who hath subjected the same in hope. Because the creature itself also shall be delivered from the bondage of corruption, into the glorious liberty of the children of God. For we know that the whole creation groaneth and travaileth in pain together until now: And not only they, but we ourselves also, which have the first fruits of the spirit, even we ourselves, groan within ourselves waiting for the adoption, the redemption of our body."

In order to make this passage of scripture have the least appearance of asserting universal salvation; the *creature* and the *whole creation* * must mean rational *creatures only*; of which there is not the least evidence: But that this is not the meaning, is very manifest. This word, which is used four times in these verses, is found in fifteen other places; and does not appear to mean rational creatures only, except in two places. ‖ It is used twice in the first Chap. of this epistle, v. 20, 25, where it means the visible creation, and creatures in general, as it also does in the 39th v. of this chap. And that by *the creation*, in this passage, is meant, not man, but the visible, material creation, and the various inferior creatures, subjected to man, and abused by him, is evident: 1. Because the creature is said to be made subject to vanity, *not willingly*; which cannot be true of those who are *voluntary* servants of sin; which all men are, except those who are the sons of God. 2. The creature or creation is here distinguished from the sons

---

* It is the same word in the original; and the passage would be more intelligible, perhaps, to the English reader, had it been translated *the creation*, in each clause of the text.

‖ Mark xvi. 15. Col. i. 23.

sons of God, v. 19, 23. So that neither the wicked, nor the children of God, are here intended by the creation.

The apostle is in this passage representing the certainty and greatness of the glory which shall take place in behalf of the church of Christ, which he had mentioned in the preceding verse, as the consequence of their present sufferings. This he does, by *first* bringing into view the church's deliverance from the power of evil and wicked men, in the latter day; when "The kingdom and dominion, and the greatness of the kingdom under the whole heaven, shall be given to the people of the saints of the most high; and they shall *reign* with Christ on earth." In order to exhibit the certainty and greatness of this event; he, by a figure often used in scripture, represents the *whole creation* as unwillingly subjected to bondage in the service of wickedness; and groaning under this calamity, and earnestly desiring and expecting deliverance; which will take place in this happy state of the church, when the creation shall be delivered out of the hands of the wicked, and consecrated and improved by saints, to the glory of God, and happiness of his children. Thus he makes the visible creation, now subjected to vanity, and in bondage to satan and wicked men, to groan, and speak a language, which is a sure and standing evidence and pledge of the future glory of the church in this world. And then in the 23d ver. he passes from this deliverance and glory of the children of God, to the yet higher and complete glory of the church, at the general resurrection, when the children of God shall shine forth as the sun in the kingdom of their Father: For which complete redemption, *not the whole creation*, but *be-*

lievers,

Sect. III.

lievers, wait and long, in this state of suffering and sin, with eager expectation. *

In this view, the connexion of these verses with the preceeding is plain and natural, and the gradation observed, clear and beautiful.—Here is not a word in favor of universal salvation; but the whole is perfectly consistent with what this apostle asserts in this chapter, and the next, and elsewhere, viz. That they who live after the flesh *shall die*; and that God, willing to shew his wrath, and make his power known, endureth with much long suffering these vessels of wrath, *fitted to destruction.* Who shall be punished with *everlasting destruction*, &c.

Eph. i. 10. " That in the dispensation of the fulness of times, he might gather together in one all things in Christ, both which are in heaven, and which are on earth, even in him." Col. i. 20. " And having made peace through the blood of his cross, by him to reconcile all things unto himself, by him, I say, whether they be things in earth, or things in heaven."— These words have been produced by some, as containing the doctrine of universal salvation; as *all things*, which are in heaven and on earth, are here said to be gathered together in one, and to be reconciled unto God by Christ, which, they say, certainly must comprehend *all men*.

Answer.

* When it is said, ver. 21. " The creation itself shall be delivered from the bondage of corruption, *into* the glorious liberty of the children of God;" the meaning is, that the visible creation, which is now abused to answer the purposes of the enemies of God, shall be delivered from this bondage, in itself so undesirable, *in* the deliverance, and glorious liberty and triumph of the church, in the latter days, and for the sake of the children of God. The word here translated *into*, is many times in this epistle, and in other places, translated *in*, *for*, *to*, and *unto*.

Sect. III.

Answer 1. By gathering together, in one, *all things* in Christ; or, as it might be rendered, gathering all things together under one head, is doubtless meant, setting Christ at the head of all things in heaven and earth, i. e. on the throne of the universe, having the government and direction of all things put into his hands: Or, as he himself expresseth it, Matth. xxviii. 18. "All power is given unto me, in heaven and in earth." Ch. xi. 27. "All things are delivered unto me of my Father." The whole created universe, which is expressed by heaven and earth, and the things therein, fell into a dissolved and broken state, in a sense, by the introduction of sin. Christ is appointed to bear up the pillars of it, to prevent any evil coming by sin, on the whole; and to bring the greatest good out of it, by the redemption of the church, and its attendants and consequences: And that he may effect this, all things are put into his hands, and he is made the head of all. This is expressed by the apostle in the same chap. v. 22. in different words, which serve to explain these under consideration, "And hath put *all things* under his feet, and gave him *to be head over all things* to the church." To gather together all things under one head, and to constitute Christ head over all things, is the same thing. But this does not imply the salvation of *all things*, or of all men, nor has any relation to it.

2. The other passage in the epistle to the Colossians, doubtless means much the same thing with this, and they are to be considered as parallel texts. Whoever reads these two epistles, with attention, written by St. Paul, and most probably about the same time, and compares them together, will find that much the same matter is contained in them, and often expressed in the same words with but little variation. The only difference in the words of these two parallel places is, that
in

in the former *all things in heaven and earth*, are said to be *gathered together in one*, in Christ. In the latter the same things are said to be *reconciled* by him. When all things in the created universe, which had in a measure fallen into confusion, and jarring contradictions and discord, by rebellion, were put under Christ, to be formed into one harmonious system, bringing good out of all the evil, and causing every thing to conspire to bring the greatest honor to God, and issue in the highest good of the whole; all things in heaven and earth were, in the most important and highest sense, reconciled to God, in him; and this is the same with gathering *all things* together in one, by or in Christ. Thus these passages appear to harmonize, and express one and the same thing. How can *all things*, whether they be things in earth, or things in heaven, by which more are comprehended than angels and men, and all rational creatures, be *reconciled*, in any other sense? These words, therefore, make nothing against endless punishment; but are in favor of it, and necessarily imply, it if this be most for the honor of God, and the general good; and necessary, that *all things* may be put in due order, and the most perfect harmony; which will be considered in a following section.

Some have thought the words of St. Paul, 1 Cor. xv. 22. assert the salvation of all men, "For as in Adam all die, even so in Christ shall all be made alive." But this must certainly be owing to want of proper attention to this chapter in general, and to the words which immediately precede and follow these. The apostle is here speaking of the resurrection of the body; of the resurrection of Christ, and of those who belong to him: And not a word is here said of the resurrection of any other person, but those whom Christ repeatedly promises to raise up at the last day, viz. those who in this life
believe

believe on him, Joh. vi. 40. " And this is the will of him that sent me, that every one which seeth the son, and believeth on him, may have everlasting life ; and I will raise him up at the last day." It is certain from scripture, that there shall be a resurrection of the wicked ; but this is not brought into view by the apostle in this chapter ; but he attends wholly to the resurrection of Christ and his people ; that is, the resurrection of the body. The words with which these are connected, make this sufficiently evident. " For since by man came death, by man came also the resurrection of the dead. For as in Adam all die, even so in Christ shall all be made alive. But every man in his own order; Christ the first fruits, afterwards they that are Christ's at his coming." By *death and dying* is meant the death of the body, and by resurrection, and being made alive, is meant the resurrection of the body, and that only of the saints.

The word *all* is therefore necessarily restrained here to all that belong to Christ. When it is said, In Adam *all* die ; it means all that are in Adam, all his posterity ; and when it is said, In Christ *all* shall be made alive, it means all that are in Christ; so that the latter *all* is not of equal extent with the former. The apostle expresseth himself here, just as he does when speaking of Adam and Christ, in that passage which has been considered, Rom. v. 18. " Therefore as by the offence of one, judgment came upon *all men* to condemnation; even so by the righteousness of one, the free gift came upon *all men* unto justification of life." It has been shewn, that by the context the words *all men* in the last clause are necessarily restrained to all those who belong to Christ, or believe in him ; and in just the same manner the word *all*, in this place, is by the context, and the matter treated of, necessarily restrained to all that
are

are Christ's, or believers in him. And they who will not attend to the context, and take these words in their only natural, plain meaning, but run away with the *meer sound* of a word or two, without considering their connexion, only to support a favorite opinion of theirs, will not understand the scriptures, but remain in darkness.

Our Saviour says, Joh. xii. 32. "And I, if I be lifted up from the earth, will draw *all men* unto me." It has hence been inferred with great assurance, by some, that every one of the human race will be saved by Christ.

This is the *only word* which Christ spake when he was on earth, in favor of universal salvation, if this be so: And this had need be very plain, and strongly asserted here, and so that the words cannot possibly be understood in any other sense; to counterbalance all that has been quoted from him, in which the contrary is asserted over and over again, in the most plain and unequivocal terms. One design of Christ's coming into the world was to reveal the true character of God; to proclaim the love of God and his designs of mercy to men, and what would be the issue of all this to mankind. And if his grand design was to save *every man*, and this were necessary for the full and most glorious display of the divine character, it might have been expected that he would dwell much upon this glorious theme, *the salvation of all*, and set it in a light most clear and incontestible. But the fact is so far from this, that he dwelt abundantly on the future and everlasting punishment of the wicked; and set it in the most alarming, dreadful light; representing it by being cast into *a furnace of fire*; into *a fire that never shall be quenched*; *where their worm dieth not, and the fire is not quenched*; and dwells long upon it, repeating it again and again. And he leads us to the day of judgment, and represents himself as dooming the wicked, even all who were not

friendly

friendly to him in this world, to *everlasting fire*; and concludes by saying, *These shall go away into everlasting punishment.* And he has not left the least hint to caution us against understanding him as asserting the endless punishment of the wicked; nor has he spoken one sentence, that any one pretends has the least appearance of a contrary meaning, unless it be this. If when this is carefully examined, it should appear to assert, that every man that ever did, or shall exist, shall be saved, and cannot be fairly understood in any other sense; we shall be thrown into an inextricable plunge, by finding a most astonishing inconsistency!

But there will appear no danger of falling into such a difficulty; and an easy and natural sense will be found in these words, consistent with the endless punishment of the wicked, by attending to the following observations.

1. These words of Christ evidently respect the consequence of his crucifixion, *in this world*, and while men are *in this life*; and it is a *forced* sense indeed, to suppose they respect every person that had ever lived, and was then in the unseen world; or that he means to say, that though men live in unbelief through life, he will draw them to himself, and they shall be converted *after they die.* The words of Christ respecting the same thing, serve fully to explain these, Joh. iii. 14, 15. "As Moses lifted up the serpent in the wilderness; even so must the Son of man be lifted up; that *whosoever believeth in him*, should not perish, but have eternal life." Here Christ tells how men should be drawn to him, viz. by believing on him, and all that do not believe on him, are represented as certainly *perishing*.

2. The words *all*, and *all men*, are used, when every individual is not intended, but *many* or all in general, or a great multitude. There are the following instances

of this; and many more that might be mentioned. Matth. iii. 5, 6. "*All* Judea, and *all* the region round about Jordan went out to John, and were baptized of him in Jordan." Mark xi. 32. "*All men* counted John, that he was a prophet indeed." It is said *all men* came to Chrift, Joh. iii. 26. Mark i. 37. The difciples fay to Chrift, "*All men* feek after thee." They do not mean *every man* without exception; for that was not true.

The words *all men* are fometimes ufed for the gentile nations in general, in oppofition to the Jews only; and to fignify, that the gofpel and falvation were not confined to the latter; but equally extended to the former; though *every man* be not included. Our Saviour fpeaks the words under confideration, at an interview which he had with a number of *Greeks*, profelytes to the worfhip of the true God, from among the Gentiles, who had came up to Jerufalem to worfhip at the feaft; and, upon their defire, were introduced to him, by his difciples. Thefe words are fpoken with reference to them; and are fuited to convey this idea to them, viz. That after his death, of which he fpeaks in the preceding verfes, falvation by him fhould be extended to the gentile nations, as well as to the Jews; and they fhould be drawn unto him: And *not* that he would actually fave every one of the human race; for fuch a thought could not be fuggefted to them by thefe words. Nor have we now any warrant to put fuch a *forced* meaning on them, when another, confiftent with all that Chrift has faid of everlafting punifhment, is fo natural and eafy.

3. Salvation by Chrift is not only extended to all nations, but the influence of the gofpel will continue and fpread, till all men in general, if not every individual perfon then living, fhall be drawn to Chrift, and become his friends and fervants. This event is fo much

and

and so often predicted in the scriptures, that none who attend to them properly can be ignorant of it. Christ represents this, by a woman putting leaven into three measures of meal, which continues there, till *the whole is leavened*; and by many other similitudes, all importing, that the gospel of the kingdom shall be preached and spread in the world, till, by the divine influence attending it, all nations, the whole world, or *all men*, shall be brought into subjection to him; and the kingdoms of this world shall become the kingdom of Christ. "The Lord will make bare his holy arm in the eyes of *all nations*, and *all* the ends of the earth shall see the salvation of God." Isai. lii. 10. "And they shall *all* know the Lord, from the least of them, unto the greatest of them." Jer. xxxi. 34. In the 22d Psal. where the death of Christ is predicted, the consequence of this is expressed in the following words; "*All the ends of the world* shall remember, and turn unto the Lord; and *all the kindreds of the nations* shall worship before thee." These words, and those of our Saviour, under consideration, express the same event, and illustrate each other. Who then can think they imply the actual salvation of all the human race?

Another passage of scripture, which has been produced, as favouring the doctrine of universal salvation, is 1 Pet. iii. 18, 19, 20. Speaking of Christ, he says, "Being put to death in the flesh, but quickened by the spirit: By which also he went and preached unto the spirits in prison; which sometime were disobedient, when once the longsuffering of God waited in the days of Noah, while the ark was preparing."

A few observations on these words, will be sufficient to shew, that there is nothing in them favourable to the salvation of all men; but directly the contrary.

1. Granting, that Christ did go and preach to the
spirits,

spirits, when they were in prison, either before or after his resurrection, though it is not asserted in these words; for this was done by the spirit, and they might be preached to *before* they were spirits in prison: Yet, granting as above, we are not told, *what he preached.* He might preach no glad tidings, and nothing but terror and eternal damnation to them, consistent with all that is said here.

2. If it be granted, that he preached the gospel to them, we are not told what was the effect; or that so much as one of them repented and believed, and was delivered out of prison. They may all be in prison yet, notwithstanding any thing that is said here; and consequently, be more miserable forever, than if they had not heard this preaching.

3. Granting, not only that Christ did preach to them *when in prison*; and that he preached the gospel to them, and offered to deliver and save all of them; but that they all accepted the offer, and are gone to heaven; all which is only matter of mere conjecture, as neither of these is asserted, or implied in this passage: But granting them all, it does not follow from hence, that all the rest of mankind, who die in their sins, or that so much as one, except those who lived in the days of Noah, will be saved. But the contrary may be very strongly inferred: For if all that had died in their sins, from the beginning of the world to the death of Christ, were to be saved, why are those who perished by the flood singled out from all the rest, and the preaching of Christ confined to them? This looks as if they were to be distinguished from all others, who are left in prison, without hope of deliverance.

This text therefore appears to be a poor, sandy foundation for a man to build his hopes of salvation upon, or of the salvation of others: Yea, he must be infatuated to a great degree, who has the least dependence on this

for

Sect. III.

for his deliverance from hell, and obtaining eternal salvation.

4. When the most easy, plain meaning of these words is fixed, it will very clearly appear, that they have no reference to the salvation of any one that ever did, or shall die in his sins; but imply the contrary to this.

It is not here said that these spirits were in prison, when Christ went, and, by the spirit, preached unto them. They were spirits in prison when this epistle was written; but were once imbodied spirits, the spirits of those long since disobedient men, who lived in the days of Noah; to whom he, inspired by Christ to foretell the flood, and warn and exhort them to prepare for it, was a preacher of righteousness for one hundred and twenty years. Through which space the spirit of Christ did strive with them, and the longsuffering of God waited upon them. All this is exactly agreeable to the history of the flood, and its attendants. Noah was inspired to warn that generation in words, by foretelling the flood; and by actions, in building the ark; and the spirit of God did strive with them during this time: But they were disobedient to all his warning and preaching; and consequently perished in their sins: And their spirits are confined in the prison of hell, where Christ fixeth the rich man when he died; and are kept in custody, as the fallen angels are, unto the judgment of the great day.

And that this is the true sense of this passage, is confirmed by the apostle's evident design. It is introduced to encourage and animate christians to faithfulness, patience, constancy, and cheerful resolution, in following Christ, under all opposition and suffering from wicked men. He mentions the sufferings of Christ, and his triumphant resurrection and deliverance; and then introduces this instance of Noah, and those with whom he lived

before

before the flood, who opposed him, and the spirit of Christ, preaching to them by him. God waited on them with long suffering; and Noah went through his suffering and work with patience and resolution; till at length, the time of vengeance came; when Noah and his family were saved; but the disobedient were destroyed; not by ceasing to exist; for though their bodies perished, their souls were shut up in the prison of hell, where they now were, and had been above two thousand years; not as prisoners of hope, but of justice, reserved unto judgment, and final, eternal condemnation. This representation is suited to support and encourage Christians, while they were ridiculed and opposed, and suffering by wicked men, in the midst of a crooked and perverse nation; and to excite them, with patience and meekness, to wait the expected end. St. Peter makes use of this instance to the like purpose, in his second epistle, in the following words, "For if God spared not the old world, but saved Noah, the eighth person, a preacher of righteousness, bringing in the flood upon the world of the ungodly; the Lord knoweth how to deliver the godly out of temptations, and to reserve the unjust unto the day of judgment, to be punished." And by the way, if the ungodly men, who perished by the flood, were delivered and carried to heaven by Christ, so long before the day of judgment, they could not be a fit instance of God's reserving wicked men unto the day of judgment to be punished, and it was not to the apostle's purpose: But if they were then in the prison of hell, reserved in confinement, unto judgment, to be punished with a severity becoming their guilt and wickedness; this example is mentioned agreeable to truth, and is suited to answer his end.

On the whole, therefore, there is not the least evidence

dence from these words of St. Peter, that any one man that has died, or shall die in his sins, ever was, or ever will be delivered from a state of punishment, to all eternity: But the whole that he says has a different and contrary complexion, viz. That men who are disobedient to Christ, while they live in this world, are cast into the prison of hell when they die; and are kept there in custody, unto the day of judgment; when they shall receive of Christ, the judge, according to what they have done *in the body*, and be doomed to a more severe and everlasting punishment.

Rev. v. 13. " And every creature which is in heaven, and on earth, and under the earth, and such as are in the sea, and all that are in them, heard I, saying, Blessing, and honor, and glory, and power, be unto him that sitteth upon the throne, and unto the Lamb, forever and ever." These words have been produced by some, as a proof that *all men* and devils will be happy, and praise God, and Christ forever and ever. How far they are from proving any such thing, will appear, if it be considered:

1. John saw this take place, and heard this universal song of praise, when Christ took the government of the world into his hands; being made head over all things to the church; represented by his taking the book out of the right hand of him who sat upon the throne, in order to open the seals of it, and accomplish the divine decrees contained in it, in the administration of providence, to the end of the world. This therefore can have no reference to the winding up and issue of things, at the day of judgment, or in any after period; and consequently can have no respect to the final salvation of all, or of any. And long after this scene, when all the seals of the book were opened, John saw all the devils, and all the men who died in their sins, cast into

a lake of fire; where they were to be tormented forever and ever: And he certainly had no vision before, or after, which is contrary to this, or looks beyond it.

2. If these words are any proof of the salvation of all men, they are an equal proof, that *every creature* on earth, and under the earth, and in the sea, *and all that are in them*, both beasts, serpents, worms, and fishes, will actively sing praise to God; becoming reasonable creatures, and having the faculty of speech, and will be happy in this employ forever. But there are very few, if any, who will believe all this to be asserted here. Therefore a more natural, consistent meaning offers itself, and must be the only true one.

3. This is only a figurative representation, to express the universal subjection of *all things* to the power and government of Christ; to be improved to answer his ends, and to promote his blessedness, honor and glory; and the happiness of this desirable, joyful event, and his worthiness to receive all this. This is parallel to the frequent representations in the prophets and in the psalms, where mountains, hills and trees, beasts and cattle, fire and hail, stormy wind, dragons, and *all the works of creation*, are represented as praising God! How absurd would it be to infer from this, that all things were rational, and capable of praising God in an active way, or ever will be? All the creation praises God, as the divine glory and character are exhibited by every creature; but in this all creatures and things are passive, except those which are rational, and the friends of God. They are the priests, who actively offer up this praise to God; for which, all his works of creation and providence afford the most ample matter. In this sense, "The wrath of man shall praise God." Psal. lxxvi. 10. All the rebellion of creatures he will turn to his own highest honor and praise: And if it be necessary,

in order to this, that there should be endless punishment, which may be true, and the evidence, that it is so, is to be exhibited hereafter; then this punishment, and those that shall be punished forever, shall render an eternal tribute of praise to God, which otherwise could not have been obtained. In this view, the words under examination are so far from implying, that all creatures, or all men, shall be happy forever, that the contrary is necessarily implied, viz. That creatures will be punished without end; even as many as shall be necessary for God's highest honor and praise. The smoke of their torment shall rise up in the sight of all happy intelligences, and bring a tribute of praise to God, which shall be actively offered up to him, by those who are his happy friends. See Rev. xix. 1, &c.

Psal. cxlv. 9. The Lord is good unto all, and his tender mercies are over all his works." 1 Joh. iv. 8, 16. "God is love." It is said the character these words give of God, is inconsistent with his making any of his creatures miserable forever.

Answer 1. This is not inconsistent with his punishing them, and inflicting very great evil and misery upon them. This we know he has done in this world. He destroyed the inhabitants of the old world with a flood. He burnt up the inhabitants of Sodom and Gomorrah with fire and brimstone. He overthrew Pharaoh and his army in the red sea. He destroyed the inhabitants of Canaan by fire and sword; and he inflicts all the evils that nations or individuals have suffered in this world; of which there are instances innumerable, and many of them very dreadful and terrible. The Psalmist says, in the words preceding those just quoted, "Men shall speak of the might of thy *terrible acts*." In Psal. lxvi. 3, &c. are the following words, "Say unto God, *how terrible art thou* in thy works! Come and see the works of God; *he is terrible* in his doing toward the children of men." And he is often ſtiled, *The great and terrible God, with whom is terrible majeſty.* And if all this be conſiſtent with his goodneſs to all, and with his tender mercies being over all his works; then any degree and duration of puniſhment, which his creatures deſerve, may be conſiſtent with it, notwithſtanding any thing we know. Can any man preſcribe to God, and point out the exact meaſure of evil, and the length of the puniſhment creatures may ſuffer, conſiſtent with his goodneſs?

Anſ. 2. God may be good to *all*, and his tender mercies be over all his works; and yet puniſh his creatures with endleſs miſery. Where is there *one*, who has not experienced the goodneſs of God? Let him be pointed out, if there be one. In this world, of which the Pſalmiſt evidently ſpeaks, and not of the inviſible world, every one who has lived, does now, or ever will live, receives great and conſtant kindneſs from God; for every thing better than perfect miſery, is goodneſs and tender mercy to ſinners.*

Anſ. 3. Though God be L O V E, infinite, unbounded goodneſs; yet this is not only conſiſtent with his puniſhing creatures according to their deſerts; but his great love and goodneſs may influence him to puniſh them without end; and not to do it, may be inconſiſtent with infinite goodneſs.

It is not thought inconſiſtent with the greateſt benevolence and compaſſion, in an earthly king or judge, to ſentence a criminal to a moſt painful death; and to ſee it executed, when the ſufferer deſerves it, and this is

---

* Some render the original words thus, "His tender mercy is *above* all his works." That is, his work of mercy in the redemption of ſinners, is his chief and higheſt work. So it is tranſlated in the Septuagint, and by others.

is necessary for the public good : Yea, this is not only *consistent* with the most extensive and unblemished goodness; but is itself an exercise and act of love and goodness; because the public and general good is sought and promoted by it. And it is the nature of true, and the most exalted love and benevolence, to regard the good of the public; and not to give that up, and act contrary to it, in order to favor an unworthy individual. To do this is partiality, which is contrary to uprightness and goodness. Yea, to spare the criminal from just punishment, in such a case, would be so far from the dictates and fruit of love, that it would be an act of unrighteousness and cruelty; to injure the public, and hurt millions, in order to grant an undeserved favor to any individual. Should a king spare his own son from a just punishment, when the good of the public required that it should be inflicted, and thereby ruin the whole kingdom; this would be the height of injustice and cruelty. *

If

* And his causing his son to be punished, would be so far from an act of cruelty, that it would be an act of mercy; and perfectly consistent with love and tender compassion for his son. Yea, it would be an evidence of *his true benevolence to his son,* as it would be the strongest evidence of his love to the public : For true love to the community, necessarily implies benevolence to every individual of which the community is composed.

The following words of Cicero, the famous Roman orator, in his fourth oration against Cataline, who was at the head of a conspiracy, formed to destroy the city and the the principal men in it, are worthy to be introduced here.

"For let me ask, Should a master of a family, finding his "children butchered, his wife murdered, and his house "burnt by a slave, inflict upon the offender a punishment "that fell short of the highest rigor; would he be counted "mild and merciful, or inhuman and cruel? If we punish "them" that is the conspirators, "with the utmost severity,

"we

If God be infinitely good, he must and will punish those creatures who deserve it, with endless punishment, when this is necessary for the highest good and happiness of his kingdom; for this is the dictate of the most perfect love; and not to do it, would be inconsistent with goodness. If this be so, in vain is the love and goodness of God alledged, as inconsistent with endless punishment. That the highest good of God's eternal kingdom does not require that such a punishment should be inflicted, it is certain, no man has any right or ability to determine; and the evidence which there is of the contrary, will be considered in the next section.

These are the chief and leading passages of scripture, which have been thought by the advocates for universal salvation to be most clearly inconsistent with endless punishment. And let every one now judge, whether they are sufficient to overbalance those which have been produced in the preceding section, as plainly declaring, in a variety of ways, that the future punishment of the wicked will be endless; so that he can sit down with satisfaction and confidence, and rest his eternal interest on this foundation, and rejoice in the prospect of everlasting happiness, purely because the scripture says that *all* shall be happy forever, whatever be their character, and however they live in this world. Yea, let all judge, whether these texts have the *least weight* in opposition to eternal punishment, and are not perfectly consistent with that doctrine. Surely this may be easily decided. Greater light and evidence cannot be desired; and divine revelation has set this point in so clear a light, that he who runs may read, if he have eyes to see.

SECTION

" we shall be accounted *compassionate*; but if we are remiss in
" the execution of justice, we may deservedly be charged
" with the *greatest cruelty*, in exposing the public and our
" fellow citizens to ruin."

SECTION IV.

WHEREIN it is considered, what reason *may be given for the Doctrine of endless Punishment, which is revealed in the Holy Scriptures: Or,* why God will punish impenitent Sinners forever: *And whether there be any* reasonable objections *against this.*

THOUGH it be granted that reason, without the help of divine revelation, can determine nothing, with certainty about future and endless punishment: Yet, when we find the doctrine of eternal punishment expresly and abundantly asserted in the Bible, we may reason upon it; and as it must be most reasonable, it may *appear* to be so, and we be able to vindicate it from all objections which any may pretend to found in reason against it. It will therefore be proper and useful to consider this doctrine in the light of reason, and see how far it may be vindicated on this ground; and whether the objections that are made against it can be supported by reason.

Not a few have been so prejudiced against this doctrine, by their inclination and feelings, and their own way of reasoning on the subject, that they come to the Bible determined not to find it there, or if they do, to reject that book as not from God. And some professed Christians have been so weak and unreasonable, as to think they have been doing God service, in attempting to prevent persons of this cast renouncing the Bible, and becoming professed Deists, by trying to make it appear, that it contains no such doctrine.

A contrary method is here proposed, viz. To examine their reasonings and objections, and see whether they

they will bear the test of truth and sound reason; or are only the figments of a dark and prejudiced mind.

FIRST, Let it be inquired, Whether God may *justly* punish any of his rebellious creatures with an endless punishment; or whether they can deserve such a punishment?

If sin against God be so great a crime as fully to deserve an endless punishment, so that his justice and righteousness may be gloriously displayed by inflicting it; then this may be one reason why he will do it. But if not; if such a punishment be too great, and exceeds the ill desert of the sinner; it is impossible he should be doomed to it by the righteous Governor of the world.

It has been said, that endless punishment is truly an *infinite evil*, and therefore cannot be justly inflicted on any, unless their crimes, or their guilt, be infinitely great; for justice in punishing consists in proportioning the punishment to the magnitude of the crimes, for which it is inflicted: But no finite creature, especially man, can contract infinite guilt, or be guilty of crimes infinitely great, in the short space of human life; therefore cannot deserve an infinite or endless punishment.

Let impartial reason be consulted on this point. If it can be made evident and certain, that sin against God is not an infinite evil, a crime of unbounded magnitude, the argument in favour of endless punishment from the reason of the thing must be given up; and it must be acknowledged, that no reason can be offered why God should punish the sinner forever. ‖ But if sin

‖ It will be thought by some, perhaps, that too much is granted here; and that God's punishing the sinner without end may be vindicated as just and proper, though the infinite evil of sin be denied.

There have been those, it must be acknowledged, who have

Sect. IV.

sin be an infinite evil, a crime so great that it really has, in one or more respects, no bounds or limits, and this shall appear to be agreeable to the dictates of reason and common sense; when it must be acknowledged, that it deserves an endless punishment, and that this is the proper wages of all sin against God; and therefore he may with justice and propriety inflict it; and must do it, whenever he lays judgment to the line, and righteousness

have rejected the doctrine of the infinite evil or ill desert of sin, as not to be vindicated, and involving unanswerable difficulties, in that view; and yet have thought they could give a good reason, why they who die in their sins should be punished forever, viz. Because they will continue to sin, and remain in a state of rebellion without end; and therefore will deserve to be punished without end; and this will be proper, and even necessary.

But perhaps, when this is examined, it will not appear to have any weight, or agreeable to scripture or reason. For,

1. The scripture represents sinners to be sentenced to this punishment, and punished in the future state, for the sins which they did commit, *when in the body*, in this world. When our Saviour represents himself as sentencing sinners to endless punishment, the sentence is grounded on their past conduct, in this world, "For I was an hungred, and ye gave me no meat, &c." And St. Paul says, "We must all appear before the judgment seat of Christ; that every one may receive the things *done in the body*, according *to that he hath done*, whether it be good or bad." Therefore, according to scripture, sinners will be sentenced to a punishment which they already deserve, for their sins in this life; but they would not deserve to be sentenced to an endless punishment, for these sins, if they were not an infinite evil, and they infinitely criminal.

2. There does not appear to be any justice in sentencing a sinner to a punishment, which he does not *already* deserve, for what he has done; for this is to condemn him for that of which he hath not been guilty. Therefore, if the infinite evil of sin be given up, there will not appear any *justice* in endless punishment.

teoufnefs to the plummet, and rewards finners according to their works.

But when we attempt to reafon on this fubject, it ought to be done with great care and caution, left, through partiality in our own favor, we fhould reafon and judge wrong. Men have all finned againft God, and joined in a common rebellion; and this is naturally attended with a felfifh partiality, difpofing them to overlook their own guilt, and call in queftion the righteoufnefs of their Maker's conduct, if he treats them according to their defert. Therefore, however juft it may appear to an impartial judge, that rebellious creatures fhould be punifhed forever; yet, no wonder if the heart of rebels fhould rife againft it, and fo far prejudice their minds, as to blind them to the reafonablenefs of it, and lead them to pronounce it unjuft. The danger of error here lies chiefly on this fide.

Whether fin be an infinite evil, and in what fenfe it is fo, will appear, it is hoped, by attending to the following obfervations, objections and anfwers.

1. All fin, or wrong affection and conduct of men, is more or lefs criminal, according as their obligations to the contrary are greater or lefs; or, according to the degree of obligation that is violated, is the degree and magnitude of the crime in violating fuch obligation. There are different degrees of obligation. A man is under greater obligation to love and befriend his parents, wife and children, or his benevolent friend, from whom he has received innumerable kindneffes; than he is to a ftranger, or one who has no peculiar relation to him. Therefore, if he is unkind and injurious to the former, this is an unfpeakably greater crime in him, than his unkind and injurious treatment of the latter can be.

2. The obligations which men violate by fin, or wrong

wrong affection or conduct, are chiefly derived from the object who is thereby oppofed and injured: Therefore, the chief aggravation of all fin, or the greatnefs of the crime, is derived from the object, againft which it is committed; and is according to the greatnefs, excellence, worth and importance of that object, and the criminal's fpecial concern and connexion with it, &c. There are indeed other confiderations which may render obligation, in particular inftances, greater or lefs, and confequently, the magnitude of the crime in violating the obligation, will be in fome refpects varied by thefe: But the *chief* and higheft aggravation of all fin has its foundation in the object againft which it is committed, and the evil of it chiefly confifts in this.

Hence it is a greater crime for a fon to hate and injure, and act a cruel part towards his excellent father, who prefides in a large family with dignity and benevolence, and who alone provides for him, and all the reft; than it would be, for him to treat one of the fervants in the family after the fame manner. If a man fall upon a ftranger, whom he meets in the road, and takes away his life, in order to obtain his money, his crime is great: But if he proceed to take away the life of his moft worthy friend and greateft benefactor, who had often refcued him from death; this would be a crime immenfely greater than the former. He is very criminal who injures, and feeks to deftroy, and actually takes away the life of one of his inoffenfive, though moft inconfiderable neighbours: But how much more criminal and ill deferving is he, who rifes in rebellion againft a moft excellent prince, on whom a great nation depend for protection, fupport and happinefs; and actually dethrones him, and puts him to death, and hereby brings total ruin on his whole kingdom?

Concerning fuch inftances as thefe, the commonfenfe, the

S   feelings

Sect. IV.   (124)

feelings of men determine without hesitation, and even irresistibly, without the labor of long reasoning; they being, in a sense, *selfevident*. And doubtless, if men had as clear discerning, and as great sensibility, respecting the being and character of God, his presence, greatness, power, excellence, goodness, &c. and of the absolute dependence of all things on him, and of the infinite importance of his being and kingdom, as they have, with respect to those things mentioned in the examples above; the conviction of the infinite magnitude of the crime of rebelling against him would be more than equally clear and irresistible.

In all the instances mentioned, and in all of this kind that can be imagined, the greater guilt and ill desert of the criminal arises from the object injured, against which the crime is committed; and is in proportion to the degree of obligation violated by the transgressor.

3. All the sins of men are committed against God: He is opposed and injured thereby. This cannot be disputed, since sin is a transgression of the law of God; for to disregard, oppose and despise the law of God, is certainly to disregard, oppose and despise God, and to rise in rebellion against his authority and government. Some instances of sin are *more directly* against God, than others; but all sin is against him, and he is the chief object who is opposed and injured by it; because he is the first and the greatest; and so much exceeds all others, who can be injured by sin, in his being, worth, and extensive rights and interest, that, in comparison with him, they are of no consideration, sink into nothing, and vanish. This is strongly expressed by David, when he was humbling himself before God for his sins. "Against thee, *thee only*, have I sinned, and done this evil in *thy sight*."

4. God is infinitely great, excellent, and worthy; and his being, interest, honor and kingdom, are of
infinite

infinite worth and importance. His interest is so great, extensive and universal, that, strictly speaking, there is no other interest, but *this One*, in the universe. He has made all things *for himself:* He is the only proprietor, who has an absolute, perfect, and unalienable right to all creatures and things. They all depend wholly and constantly on him; and he is the boundless, infinite benefactor to all: His authority over all is without limits, and his government absolutely perfect.

Therefore, all sin is against an infinitely great, worthy and important object; it is opposition to God, his whole interest and kingdom; it disregards and despises him, and tramples his authority under foot.

From these premises, which none can dispute, but all must grant, the plain and unavoidable conclusion is, that all sin is infinitely criminal and ill deserving. This proposition is as demonstrably certain, as any one of a moral nature can be. If wrong affection and conduct be criminal, in proportion to the greatness of the obligation to the contrary; and the obligation be great in proportion to the greatness and worthiness of the object injured by such wrong affection and conduct: If all sin be against God and injurious to him; and he is infinitely great and worthy, and his interest and kingdom infinitely great and important; all which is granted: Then men are under infinite obligations to God, to love and serve him, and be friendly to his interest and kingdom; consequently all opposition to these, is a violation of infinite obligation, and infinitely criminal.

Or shorter thus:

Every crime is great in degree, in proportion to the greatness and worthiness of the being, against which it is committed. Every sin is committed against God, and is an injury done to him, who is infinitely great and worthy: Therefore every sin is a crime of infinite magnitude, and deserves an infinite punishment. 5.

5. The infinite evil of sin appears from the evil consequence of it, or the evil which it naturally tends to produce, and will take place, unless prevented. A crime is great in proportion to the evil it tends to effect, or is the natural consequence of it. But the evil which sin aims at, and tends to produce, is truly infinite.

This appears from what has been already observed. All sin is against God, and his whole interest and kingdom: It tends to dishonor and dethrone the Almighty; to destroy all his happiness, and to ruin his whole interest and kingdom; to introduce the most dreadful confusion and infinite misery, and render the whole universe infinitely worse than nothing, to all eternity. If there be any such thing as *infinite evil*, this is such; and he who aims at this, and does the least towards it, or what has a direct tendency to it, is guilty of a crime which has no bounds, in this respect, as to its degree of ill desert. It is big with infinite mischief, and therefore is in itself an infinite evil; and nothing short of endless punishment can be its proper reward. To inflict an evil infinitely less than this, as a punishment, falls infinitely short of being answerable to the crime, or of manifesting the evil or guilt of it.

To this it will be objected, perhaps, that no such evil actually takes place. God cannot be dethroned, or really hurt, by the sinner; he is infinitely beyond the reach of the rebel; and his kingdom and interest cannot be hurt: Yea, God will over-rule all sin for his own honor, and to promote the happiness and glory of his kingdom forever. Why then should the sinner be punished, as if he had actually effected infinite evil, when the evil tendency of what he does, and his criminal endeavours are prevented taking effect, and no such evil can come?

Answer 1. The crime is not to be estimated by the evil

evil that is actually effected by it; but by the nature and tendency of what is done, and the aim of the criminal. Though the evil confequence be prevented, and it be not in the power of the criminal to effect it; yet, if he does what he can to accomplish it, his crime is to be eftimated, by his manifeft difpofition, and the tendency of what he does. If a fubject attempts to take away the life of a king; or from difaffection to him, does that which tends to deftroy him, and would do it, were he not prevented; though the life of the king be not hurt, and the attempt wholly mifcarries; yet he is juftly condemned as guilty of high treafon, and punifhed accordingly.

The finner does all he can to dethrone his Maker, and render him infintiely miferable, and ruin his kingdom forever: Every fin has a ftrong and mighty tendency to this; and no thanks to the finner, that this infinite evil has not been effected, by his rebellion: And is his crime not fo great, becaufe the evil is prevented, by the infinite power and wifdom of God? He who will affert this, muft renounce all reafon and commonfenfe. David, infpired to imprecate punifhment on the wicked, fays, Pfal. xxviii. 4. "Give them *according to their deeds*, and *according to the wickednefs of their endeavours:* Give them after the work of their hands, and render to them *their defert.*" They are to be punifhed according to their deeds, the nature and tendency of them, and according to the wickednefs of their *endeavours*; whether they accomplifh what they attempt or not. Again, Pfal. xxi. 8, &c. "Thine hand fhall find out all thine enemies, thy right hand fhall find out thofe that hate thee. Thou fhalt make them as a fiery oven in the time of thine anger, &c. For they *intended evil againft thee*; they imagined a mifchievous device, *which they are not able to perform.*" According to to the objection, *their intending evil against God, and imagining a mischievous device, which they were not able to perform*, ought to have been given as a reason why they *should not* be punished; whereas it is here mentioned as a reason why God would certainly punish them.

Ans. 2. God, in punishing the wicked forever, will do no more to them, than they would have done to him, had it been in their power: And surely this is but a just and equitable punishment, which they fully deserve, if they deserve any at all. They will rebel against him, and trample on his authority and laws, let what will be the consequence, to him. He would have been dethroned, and made infinitely miserable forever, had they been able to bring it to pass: This is the tendency of their treatment of him; and this must have been the effect, had he not been able to defend himself against them, and counteract their endeavours. And do they not deserve to be treated after the same manner, by him, and made eternally miserable? Would any punishment short of this be in any measure answerable to the crime? If they have cast God behind their back, and cared nothing for his honor, interest or happiness; do they not deserve to be cast off by God, and that he should take no care of their interest or happiness? Their hearts have been full of mischievous devices against God, and all they have done has tended to destroy him, his happiness and kingdom: And will it not be just to bring the mischief on their own heads, and give them over to endless misery? Among the laws given by Moses to Israel, is the following one: Deut. xix. 16. &c. "If a false witness rise up against any man to testify against him that which is wrong; the judges shall make diligent inquisition: And behold, if the witness be a false witness, and testified falsely against his brother; *then shall ye do unto him, as he had thought to have done*

done unto his brother. And thine eye shall not pity, but life shall go for life, eye for eye, tooth for tooth, hand for hand, foot for foot." This law requires them to punish the man, who, by false witness, thought and endeavoured to bring evil on his brother, by inflicting that very evil on him, though his brother received not the least hurt by it. All will doubtless say, this is a righteous law; and it is but just that such an evil designing man should be thus punished. And will it be unrighteous in God, who ordered this law, to act by the same rule, in punishing those who have born false witness against him and his character; and have attempted to bring ruin on him and all his friends; by giving them up to eternal destruction; though he and his kingdom have received no hurt by their wicked attempts?

As God and his kingdom are infinitely distinguished from every thing else, in their infinite greatness, excellence, and importance; so rebellion against him, and opposition to his interest and kingdom, and an attempt to destroy the whole, must be equally distinguished from any other possible or supposable crime; and therefore it is right and proper, that it should have an equally distinguished punishment; that is, an endless one. A temporary punishment, which is infinitely less than this, and infinitely less than the evil of sin, cannot answer the end of punishment; it will neither express the evil or crime of injuring the infinitely great JEHOVAH, nor serve in the least degree to shew his infinite worth, grandeur and greatness; but speak a contrary language, viz That his being, character and kingdom, are of infinitely less worth, than they really are; and so would be a real dishonor to him.

If one who has defamed the character of a worthy personage, being prosecuted, convicted and condemned, should be punished only by paying a small fine, viz. one penny

penny or shilling: The language of this would be, that the character of the person defamed was worth no more; and therefore would be so far from answering to the injury, and wiping off the reproach; that it would really fasten the disgrace upon him, and his character would suffer more, than if the criminal had not been condemned and punished. And if God should punish rebels against him, who have defamed him and highly injured his character, with a temporary punishment only, this would be as far from answering to his infinitely superior, excellent and important character, and properly vindicating it, as if no punishment at all were inflicted: Yea, it would be infinitely worse than none, and really degrade his character, and be a reproach to him. In this case, a *just punishment* must be answerable to the infinitely amiable, worthy and important character, which is injured and blasphemed; that is, such a punishment as is suited to express the greatness of the injury done, and the infinite worthiness of him who is injured, and thus take off the reproach cast upon him. But this can be no less than an endless punishment. Therefore such a punishment is *just*, it is deserved, and must be inflicted, if there be any punishment at all, in order to vindicate the Divine character.

But there are other objections against the infinite evil of sin, and the sinner's desert of endless punishment, which must be considered.

Obj. 1. It is said, that as all creatures are *finite*, they are not capable of infinite guilt, or of committing a crime that has an infinite degree of evil in it, or that is in any respect infinite.

Ans. 1. This objection is obviated by what has been said in proving the infinite evil of sin, viz. That this results from the greatness and excellence of the being against which it is committed; and depends not at all

on

on the degree of exiſtence of him who offers the abuſe: If a finite creature can affront and abuſe his Creator, who is infinitely great and worthy, he can be guilty of an infinite crime; becauſe the greatneſs of the injury does not ariſe from the greatneſs of him who offers it; but from the character of him who is injured.

Anſ. 2. If a creature ſhould actually put an end to his Maker's exiſtence, or dethrone him, and deſtroy his kingdom; his crime would be truly infinite, all will grant. But to deſire and attempt this, and do that which would certainly effect it, were it not prevented by a ſuperior power, is to be guilty of the ſame crime, ſo far as the criminal is concerned; and therefore muſt be infinitely great, and deſerve the ſame puniſhment, as if the effect had actually followed. The infinite magnitude of the crime, in this caſe, does not in the leaſt degree depend upon the greatneſs of the criminal, or the degree of exiſtence, of which he is poſſeſſed.

Anſ. 3. Agreeable to this, when a crime is committed, men do not firſt inquire into the greatneſs or ſmallneſs of the perpetrator, in order to determine the magnitude of the crime; but conſider the nature of the crime, and the injury done, and who is injured, &c. If an abject, dependent ſlave burns his maſter's houſe, and deſtroys him and his whole family, or attempts to do it, his inferiority and dependence on his maſter, do not extenuate his crime, in the judgment of men, but rather aggravate it: And no one will offer this as a plea in his favor, or as a reaſon for a mitigation of his puniſhment.

And here it may be obſerved, that it is equally unreaſonable, and contrary to the commonſenſe and practice of men, to ſay that an infinite crime cannot be committed in the ſhort ſpace of human life; and that men cannot deſerve endleſs puniſhment, for the ſins of a few years,

years. For as the infinity of the crime does not depend on the greatness of the offender, so neither does it depend on the length of time in which it is perpetrated. In judging of crimes, and the degree of punishment they deserve, men do not inquire what length of time was spent in committing them; but what is the nature of them, and what is done. And men are condemned to death, or imprisonment during life, for crimes which were perpetrated in a few minutes.

Obj. 2. It is said, if every sin be an *infinite* evil, a crime of infinite magnitude; then all crimes must be equal; for none can be greater than infinite: Which is contrary to reason and scripture.

Answer. This consequence does not follow from the doctrine of the infinite evil of sin, as it has been stated. Two crimes may be both infinite in their criminality, and ill desert, as committed against God; and yet, in other respects, one may be greatly aggravated and criminal above the other, being committed against more light, and greater warnings, and an abuse of greater favors, &c. They both deserve endless punishment; but one deserves *a greater degree* of punishment, than the other. It is easy to conceive two persons deserving and suffering endless punishment; and yet one deserving and suffering a much *greater degree* of pain or punishment, than the other. And is it not as easy to conceive of two persons being infinitely guilty, as rebels against the Monarch of the universe; and yet, *in other respects*, the rebellion of one be much more criminal, than that of the other? This may be illustrated by the following similitude. Two cords or cylinders extended without end, and, in this respect, both equally infinite, may be of very different diameters, and, *in that respect*, one much larger than the other.

Obj. 3. If sin be an infinite evil, because committed against an infinite object; then the virtue and holiness of creatures muſt be infinitely good, excellent and praiſeworthy, becauſe exerciſed towards the ſame infinite object; which is too abſurd to be admitted.

Anſ. This conſequence does by no means follow. Creatures can do more miſchief, by rebellion, and take more from God, than they can do good, or give to him, by their obedience. Here there is an infinite difference. It has been ſhewn, that ſin takes *all* from God, and in its very nature and tendency deſtroys all the good in the univerſe; and would actually do it, were it not counteracted by omnipotence, infinite wiſdom and goodneſs: But the obedience and holineſs of creatures is not to be eſtimated by the object towards which it is exerciſed; but by the ſubject, by him who exerciſes it, or the degree and quantity given to God. All that a finite creature can give, is but finite; He can give no more than himſelf; and therefore what he gives is infinitely ſhort of infinite, it is as nothing, compared with the object towards which it is exerciſed, or to whom it is given.

Obj. 4. Though God be infinitely great, excellent and worthy; yet finite minds can have no conception of that which is infinite. The infinity of God is altogether inconceivable to them; and out of their ſight, and all their ideas muſt be limited. But that of which they can have no idea or conception, can have no influence on the mind; and therefore cannot increaſe the obligation of creatures, ſo as to render it greater, than if the object was finite; conſequently, a creature cannot be under infinite obligations, from God's infinite greatneſs and excellence.

Anſwer. It is certainly *not true*, that a finite mind can have no conception of an infinite being, different from that which he has of one who is finite: Becauſe this is contrary to our experience, in the conſciouſneſs of the

ideas

ideas that are in our own minds. If men could have no idea of that which is infinite, different from that which they have of a finite object, they could not reason, nor speak an intelligible word about it; which the objector himself thinks he can do, and is actually doing it, while he is making the objection. And if we consult our own feelings, we find that we feel otherwise towards that which we conceive to be infinite, than we could, if we thought it was not so. The instance before us will sufficiently prove this. Are we not conscious that we ought to be affected with the infinite being and perfection of God, inexpressibly otherwise, than towards any finite being? And if so, then his *infinity*, or his being *infinitely* great and good, brings an obligation on us to respect and love him; which we could not be under, were he not infinite. And if that which is infinite, viz. infinite greatness, authority and excellence, binds us, and the greatness of the obligation arises from the infinity of the object; then it must be an infinite obligation.

When we think of future life and happiness, we easily and necessarily distinguish between temporary and endless happiness, and prefer the latter to the former, feeling, in some sense, the infinite difference. And when we attend to infinite, or endless punishment, and argue for, or against it; we feel that this is infinitely more dreadful than any finite evil, and cannot but dread it unspeakably more; and be sensible that it affords an inexpressibly stronger motive, not to rebel against God, than any finite punishment can: And that it is infinitely greater folly and madness to provoke God to cast us into such punishment, than to expose ourselves to one infinitely less. Therefore, the reason and experience of every man, if properly attended to, will teach him that the objection is without foundation.

Sect. IV.

The evidence that sin is properly an infinite evil, and has in its nature infinite ill desert, has now been considered, and objections have been examined and obviated; and the reader is to judge, whether it may not be proved, even to a demonstration, that all sin deserves infinite or endless punishment. But as the infinite evil of sin appears from another consideration, it may be further observed.

6. The atonement which has been made for sin, in order to the sinner's being pardoned, shews that there is infinite ill desert in sin.

They who acknowledge the Divinity of Christ, and consequently, his infinite greatness and worthiness, must also acknowledge, that the atonement he has made for sin, by his obedience and sufferings, has infinite worth and merit, and is as great and considerable, as the person who gave himself to be the propitiation for the sins of men. But if sin be not an infinite evil; then this atonement is infinitely more and greater than was necessary, in order to open the way for the pardon of it; and the Mediator is infinitely greater and more worthy, than it was necessary he should be, in order to make atonement for sin. One end of the atonement which Christ made for sin, was to shew what evil there is in sin, and its ill desert. But this is every way sufficient to atone for sin which has infinite ill desert; therefore, it declares sin to be an infinite evil, or to deserve infinite or endless punishment. Consequently, to deny that there is infinite evil in sin, is, in effect, to deny the Divinity of our Saviour; or the truth which is declared in the atonement which he has made for sin.

It being thus evident, beyond all contradiction, that all sin is infinitely criminal, and deserves endless punishment; so that God may justly inflict it, and must do it, if he lays judgment to the line and righteousness to the

plummet,

Sect. IV.

plummet, and punishes sinners according to their desert; it hence appears further evident and certain, that this punishment will be inflicted on all who die in their sins, from those passages of scripture which declare that God will reward them according to their works, and inflict a punishment answerable to their desert.

This is often and abundantly asserted in scripture. From many instances of this, the following are selected. Isai. iii. 11. " Wo unto the wicked, it shall be ill with him : *For the reward of his hands shall be given him.*" Psal. xxviii. 4. " Give them *according to their deeds,* and *according to the wickedness of their endeavours* ; give them *after the work of their hands, render to them their* DESERT." Matth. xvi. 27. " For the Son of man shall come in the glory of his Father, with his angels : *And then he shall reward every man according to his works.*" Rom. ii. 5, &c. " But after thy hardness and impenitent heart, *treasurest up wrath against the day of wrath,* and revelation of the righteous judgment of God ; *who will render to every man according to his deeds.* Tribulation and anguish upon every soul of man that doth evil." 2 Cor. v. 10. " For we must all appear before the judgment seat of Christ : *That every one may receive the things done in the body, according to that he hath done, whether it be good or bad.*" Rev. xx. 12. " And the dead were judged out of those things that were written in the books, *according to their works.*" xxii. 12. " Behold I come quickly ; and my reward is with me, *to give to every man according as his work shall be.*

All sin deserves endless punishment, this is the proper wages of sin, and God may most justly inflict it. God has said, in his word, that he will punish sinners in the future state, *according to their ill desert* ; therefore they will be punished forever.

SECONDLY. It must be considered, whether any good
end

end can be anfwered, by inflicting an endlefs punifhment on creatures?

If no good end can be anfwered by thus punifhing, and if it be not, all things confidered, neceffary for the good of the whole, that any creature fhould be made miferable forever; then it is not confiftent with wifdom and goodnefs to inflict fuch a punifhment upon any; though they may deferve it, and no injuftice would be done to them by inflicting it. The infinitely wife and good governor of the world always has fome wife and good end, in all he does, and never punifhes his creatures, merely for the fake of punifhing, or only to make them miferable. This is ftrongly afferted by God himfelf, when he fays. "As I live, I have no pleafure in the death of the wicked." And therefore we may be fure he will not punifh them forever, though they deferve it, unlefs it be nececeffary to prevent greater evil, and anfwer the beft and moft important purpofes.

But if endlefs punifhment, infinitely dreadful as it is, be neceffary to anfwer the higheft and beft ends, and to promote the greateft good of the whole, and is an important and effential part of the moft wife and benevolent adminiftration, in the government of the world: Then it is not only perfectly confiftent with infinite goodnefs, but it is the dictate and exercife of goodnefs itfelf; and not to inflict this punifhment, muft be infinitely difagreeable & croffing to unlimited goodnefs, & demonftrate the want of benevolence. On this fuppofition then, all the objections which have been, with fuch confidence, urged againft endlefs punifhment, from the goodnefs of God, as being inconfiftent with that, fall to the ground, and appear highly unreafonable, childifh and abfurd.

We are indeed, poor and very inadequate judges of the ends and defigns of God, in all his adminiftrations, in our present situation, and in this very imperfect and sinful state; in which it is no uncommon thing for men to call God's wisdom and goodness in question, and say, *His ways are not equal.* Therefore, though we were not able to see why there is to be endless punishment, and understand what wise and good ends God designs to answer by it; yet, since he has revealed to us, that he will punish the wicked forever, it would be very unbecoming, yea, intolerable arrogance, for men to say no good end can be answered by it, or even doubt of the wisdom and goodness of this part of the Divine administration.

But we are not left wholly in the dark, with regard to this part of God's ways. In the sober exercise of our reason, assisted by divine revelation, we are able to justify God, in punishing the wicked forever; and to see and rejoice in some of the infinitely important, wise and good ends which will be answered by this awful, tremendous branch of the Divine government, in which God will do terrible things in righteousness; so that the great good that shall be produced by it, will infinitely overbalance and swallow up all the evil.

The following considerations will be sufficient, it is presumed, to illustrate and establish this point.

I. All will grant it is not only just, that criminals should punished according to their deserts; but it is an expression of wisdom and goodness, in a governor or judge, thus to punish them, when this is suitable and necessary to maintain authority, law and government, and deter others from the like crimes. And in this case, to refuse or neglect to punish, can proceed from nothing but a defect in true benevolence and goodness. Punishments are therefore found necessary in human government, in order to prevent greater evil, and promote the public good; so that every true friend to the public, and the greatest common good, must be a friend to such punishments.

And who can think himself able to determine, that eternal punishment is not proper and necessary, as a means, to answer these ends in the Divine government, which is infinitely extended, and everlasting? And if he cannot *certainly determine* such punishment to be unnecessary and useless; he has no warrant to conclude it is not perfectly agreeable to infinite goodness, to inflict it. Why is it not as much suited, and as necessary, as a means, to restrain creatures from sin, as any kind or degree of punishments, in human governments? Who dare say, or think, that the punishment of the fallen angels, who are reserved in *everlasting* chains, under darkness, unto the judgment of the great day, has had no influence on the angels who have not sinned; and has not been a means of preserving and confirming them in obedience? And though it be certain, that the redeemed from among men will, after they are made perfect, continue in obedience and holiness forever; yet this will not be effected without means; and this may, and doubtless will be one, even the everlasting punishment of the wicked, the smoke of whose punishment will rise up in their sight forever and ever. No punishment but an endless one can answer this end. God ordered punishments in Israel, even the greatest that perhaps could be inflicted in this world, viz. That transgressors should be publicly stoned to death, that others might hear and fear, and hereby be restrained from sin. Endless punishment may be as necessary in the future state, to answer the same end.

II. It is desirable, and of the greatest importance, that all the divine perfection, his whole character and glory, even all that is amiable and excellent in God, should be acted out and displayed, in the sight of his creatures; that his friends may be under the best advantage to see it; and enjoy God, and adore and praise him forever. This is as desirable and important, as it is that God should be glorified to the highest degree; for this is done only by such a manifestation and display of his excellence and perfections, and in the consequent love and praise of his creatures: And this is as desirable and important, as the highest happiness of the servants of God, the members of his eternal kingdom; for their happiness must consist summarily in the knowledge and enjoyment of God; in beholding his glory, and loving and glorifying him. But they know and enjoy him, no further than he is manifested to them in his glorious perfection, by his works; and their happiness will be in degree answerable to this display of the Divine perfections; and is promoted by every thing, by which God is glorified.

But the eternal punishment of the wicked is suited to promote and answer these desirable and important ends; and is necessary, in order to their being accomplished, most perfectly, and to the highest degree. This will appear by descending to particulars,

1. The terrible majesty of God, and the infinite dreadfulness of his displeasure and wrath, could not be fully displayed and known, did he not inflict eternal punishment on any of his creatures who deserve it.

Terrible majesty and wrath are ascribed to God in the inspired writings, as included in his amiableness and glorious perfection, his absolutely perfect character, for which he is worthy to be loved and adored. And his terribleness and wrath are equal in degree to his infinite existence and capacity; and therefore are infinitely great & dreadful. And if it be agreeable & desirable, that there should be a God of infinite terribleness and wrath; it is equally desirable that this should *appear*, and be discovered & displayed, in the works of God. But this can not be done in any way or degree, unless it be by *terrible acts* or works, by which evil is inflicted on creatures.* If there were no possible evil in the universe, and God never did, or would inflict any evil on his creatures, as a punishment for their sins; there could be no possible appearance of terrible majesty in God, or of any displeasure and wrath; for that being from whom no evil, no pain or suffering ever did, or ever will come, has no wrath, or any thing that is terrible, or awful. And as God's terrible majesty appears, and is acted-out, only by his inflicting evil; so this appears great in proportion to the evil inflicted. Therefore infinite evil must be inflicted, in order to express the infinitely terrible majesty and wrath of God. Any finite evil or punishment will be no proper expression of infinite terribleness and wrath; but fall infinitely short of it. But endless punishment is a full and proper expression of this, as it is an evil infinitely terrible and dreadful, and can be inflicted by none but the infinitely powerful and terrible Jehovah, who only is able, in this way, to make a most glorious and eternal display of his infinite power and wrath. And is not the answering this important end, one good reason why the wicked should be punished according to their deserts? " What if God, *willing to shew his wrath*, and

make

* The *threatning* of eternal punishment against the transgressors of the law of God, is indeed an expression of infinite terror and wrath against sin, if it be supposed it may and will be executed on any: But if the punishment threatened be only a temporary one, it is no proper expression of the terrible majesty and wrath of God. And though endless punishment be threatned, yet if it be known that it will never be executed in any instance, it will stand for nothing, and be no expression of any thing terrible: Because the evil, which alone is terrible, lies in *the execution* of the threatning, and not in the threatning itself, unconnected with the punishment threatned.

make his power known, has determined to punish these *vessels of wrath*, fitted to such a destruction; to punish them with *everlasting* destruction, from the presence of the Lord and *the glory of his power?*"

2. God's infinite displeasure and anger with sin and the sinner, and the opposition of his heart to them, are properly exhibited in punishing the sinner forever; but cannot be expressed by any temporary punishment.

Infinite hatred of that which is opposition to all good, is necessarily implied in infinite benevolence and goodness; and therefore is essential to the Divine character, and it cannot be perfect and infinitely excellent without it; but directly the contrary. It is therefore desirable and necessary, that this should appear, and be gloriously displayed, in God's conduct towards sinners. One way to express this, is in punishing the sinner: But this cannot be done by any punishment, but an endless one; because the degree of hatred of sin, manifested in punishing it, is in proportion to the degree of evil inflicted, in the punishment. An endless punishment, therefore, is necessary to answer this important end. A temporary punishment will be so far from expressing infinite opposition to sin, that it expresses the contrary, viz. that God is infinitely less displeased at sin, than an infinitely perfect and good being must be; and therefore, would be worse than no punishment, and really injure the Divine character.

3. In the everlasting punishment of the wicked the infinite dignity and worthiness of God, and excellence of his law and government, are expressed and asserted in a very advantageous and striking manner, and this is one important end and design of this punishment.

Sin is criminal, and the evil of it great, in proportion to the dignity, excellence and worth of the Governor of the world, as has been shewn. Therefore, so far as the

the evil of sin is discovered; in the same degree are manifested, God's greatness, dignity, worthiness, &c. But the everlasting punishment of the sinner will be, in some respects, the strongest possible expression of the infinite evil of sin; and consequently, a bright and affecting manifestation of the infinite worthiness and excellence of God, and the sacredness of his law and government. By this punishment, it will forever appear to angels and the redeemed; yea, to all intelligences, what an infinitely evil and bitter thing it is, to sin against God; and by means of this, God will be eternally seen and exalted, in his infinite greatness, worth and excellence, as he could not be, were there no such punishment. And it will, consequently, be the occasion of joy and praise in heaven, by which God will be honored and exalted forever.

A finite punishment, which is punishing the sinner infinitely less than he deserves, would be so far from answering this end; that it would have a contrary tendency, and reflect dishonor on God, and represent him as infinitely less honorable and excellent, than he is. It hence appears, that endless punishment is as important and necessary, as is the most clear manifestation of God's infinite worthiness and glory, and his asserting and maintaining his own rights, dignity and honor, and the infinite importance and excellence of his law and government, to the greatest advantage of the universe, himself and the creation.

4. Endless punishment is suited, and necessary, to make the brightest everlasting display of the righteousness and *goodness* of God.

It has been observed, that infinite anger and displeasure against sin is essential to infinite goodness: And it must be further observed now, that such displeasure and anger is goodness itself, opposing, and kindled up into

wrath

Sect. IV.

wrath, against that which opposes and tends to destroy what infinite goodness seeks. Infinite goodness seeks the greatest good of the whole, and therefore, must be infinitely displeased with that which sets itself against all good. Therefore, the more this displeasure and anger is manifested, the greater is the manifestation of divine goodness. But this cannot be properly and fully manifested, but by inflicting infinite evil on the obstinate, confirmed enemies of all good. Hence it appears, that the greater the evil is, which is inflicted on the obstinate sinner, if it be just, the greater is the display of divine goodness; and therefore, to inflict endless punishment on such who deserve it, is a display both of the righteousness and infinite goodness of God, which could not be made in any finite punishment.

If a subject turn enemy to a whole kingdom, and do all in his power to destroy both the king and the people, and obstinately persist in his rebellion; the king must be displeased and angry, in proportion to his goodness, his benevolent regard to the highest good of his kingdom; and in this case, his goodness must be exercised and acted out, in expressing his displeasure, by punishing the obstinate offender. And to neglect to punish him, or to inflict a small and light punishment, unspeakably less than his crime deserves, would be so far from expressing any goodness, that it would demonstrate the want of it. And on the contrary, punishing him according to his desert, would be the highest evidence he could give, in this case, of his benevolence and goodness.

And why is not this equally true of the Governor of the universe? If it be, then endless punishment must be one essential part of his government, as necessary to display, in the clearest light, his infinite righteousness and goodness.

Thus

Thus it appears, from the view given of it under this head, that endless punishment will serve to manifest and display the Divine perfections and character; and in what way and manner it will do this; and why it is necessary in order to answer this infinitely important end, so much to the glory of God, and consequently for the good and happiness of all who love him.

But that infinite goodness is exercised and displayed in punishing the wicked forever, will be more fully proved under the next head; where it will be particularly considered, as it respects, and will promote the general good, the glory and happiness of the kingdom of God.

III. The eternal punishment of the wicked will, many ways, promote the highest good of the blessed, especially the redeemed from among men; and is the most proper and necessary means of their unspeakably greater degree of holiness and happiness forever, than could otherwise take place: And therefore must be agreeable to infinite goodness, and a strong expression of it.

The exercise and manifestation of God's displeasure against his enemies, and the enemies of his church and people, in condemning and punishing them according to their deserts, and evil deeds, and vindicating his servants, and their cause, and saving and delivering them from the hand and power of their adversaries, causing them to triumph over all that injured them, is certainly an instance and expression of his righteousness and goodness. The holy scriptures every where represent it in this light, of which every person, attentive to his Bible, must be sensible. God, in vindicating the righteous cause of his servants, by delivering and saving them, and manifesting his high displeasure against their enemies, by condemning and punishing them as they deserve, exercises and displays his *righteousness:* And, at the same time, this

Sect. IV.

this righteousness is nothing but kindness and mercy to his church and people. And the more his displeasure and anger towards his and their enemies is manifested, in the greatness of the righteous punishment inflicted upon them; the greater is the expression of his goodness to them; and they are unspeakably more happy in the righteousness of God, & in his love and favor to them, than they could have been, had they not been thus vindicated and delivered, and their enemies had not been destroyed and punished with everlasting destruction. Therefore the *righteousness* of God, as it respects this case, is often spoken of in scripture, as including his *goodness*; and righteousness and salvation are words frequently used as synonymous; as every careful reader of his Bible must have observed. The following passages, among a multitude of others, serve to illustrate these observations. Psal. lxxi. 2, 13, &c. " Deliver me in thy *righteousness*, and cause me to escape. Let them be confounded and consumed, that are adversaries to my soul. But I will yet *praise thee more and more*. My mouth shall shew forth thy *righteousness*, and thy *salvation* all the day." Psal. cxliii. 11, 12. " For *thy righteousness sake* bring my soul out of trouble. And of *thy mercy* cut off mine enemies, and destroy all them that afflict my soul." Psal. lxv. 5 " *By terrible things in righteousness*, wilt thou answer us, O God *of our salvation*." Deut. xxxii. 43. " Rejoice, O ye nations, his people; for *he will avenge the blood of his servants*, and will *render vengeance to his adversaries*, and *will be merciful* unto his land, and *to his people*.

Therefore the divine vengeance and eternal punishment, that shall be inflicted on the wicked, is represented in scripture to be "in the clear and full view of the redeemed and inhabitants of heaven, as a mean of exciting and greatly increasing their love, joy and praise. Psal. lii.

lii. 5, 6. Speaking of the wicked, he says, "God shall destroy thee *forever*. The righteous also *shall see*, and fear, and *shall laugh at him.*" Psal. lviii. 9, 10. "He shall take them away as with a whirlwind; both living and in his wrath. The righteous shall *rejoice when he seeth the vengeance:* He shall wash his feet in the blood of the wicked." Psal. lxxix. 12, 13. "Render unto our neighbours seven fold into their bosoms, their reproach wherewith they have reproached thee, O Lord. So we, thy people *will give thee thanks forever* Psal. xci. 8. "Only with thine eyes shalt thou behold, *and see the reward of the wicked.*" Isai. lxvi. 24. "And they shall go forth and *look upon the carcases of the men that have transgressed against me;* for their worm shall not die, neither shall their fire be quenched; and they shall be an abhorring unto all flesh." Rev. xiv. 10. "And he shall be tormented with fire and brimstone, *in the presence of the holy angels, and in the presence of the Lamb; and the smoke of their torment ascendeth up forever and ever.*" Chap. xviii. 20. "*Rejoice over her,* thou heaven, and ye holy apostles and prophets; *for God hath avenged you on her.*" Chap. xix. 1. &c. "After these things I heard a great voice of much people *in heaven,* saying, Allelujah; salvation, and glory, and honor, and power, unto the Lord our God: For true and *righteous* are his judgments; for he hath judged the great whore, which did corrupt the earth with her fornication, and *hath avenged the blood of his servants at her hand.* And again they said *Allelujah* (i. e. praise ye the Lord) and *her smoke rose up forever and ever.*"

None, surely, will dispute the goodness of God in punishing his enemies, and the enemies of his church and kingdom, so far, and as long, as shall be necessary to secure and promote the best interest, and highest happiness and glory of all who belong to this kingdom:

W   For

Sect. IV.

For that goodness itself should do this, is agreeable to common sense and reason. And this is asserted in the holy scripture. God there represents himself as giving people and nations up to ruin and destruction, for the sake of his church, as the effect and expression of his love and goodness. Isai. xliii. 3, 4. "I am the Lord thy God, the holy one of Israel, thy saviour: I gave Egypt for thy ransom, Ethiopia and Seba for thee. Since thou wast precious in my sight, thou hast been honorable, and I have loved thee: Therefore will I give men for thee, and people for thy life." In these words there is reference to the destruction of Pharaoh and the Egyptians, for the sake of Israel, that they might be delivered to the greatest advantage to themselves, as an example of what God would yet do for his church. And when we see Moses and that people rejoicing and praising God, for his goodness in overthrowing and taking vengeance on his and their enemies, in such a signal and dreadful manner, we approve of it as reasonable: For it was, viewed in all its connexions and consequences, a wonderful act of Divine goodness: Therefore it is celebrated as such; and made matter of solemn, joyful praise to God in Psal. cxxxvi. "To Him that smote Egypt in their first-born; *for his mercy endureth forever*. To Him which divided the red sea into parts, and made Israel to pass through the midst of it; for his mercy endureth forever: But overthrew Pharaoh and his host in the red sea; *for his mercy endureth forever*."

And if this was such a remarkable instance of God's goodness and mercy, thus to punish and destroy Pharaoh and the Egyptians, for the sake of his church, to promote their good and happiness; when he could have delivered them without this destruction, but not so much to his glory, and their advantage; and in this God made a display of his glorious character; and this nite goodness, a matter of admiration, joy and praise to his church, and to be celebrated forever: Then it is equally an instance of his goodness; yea, an infinitely greater and more remarkable instance of it, and proportionably brighter display of his glorious character, and greater matter of eternal joy and praise, *to punish forever* the impenitent enemies of his redeemed church; this being necessary, in order to promote their highest good, to make their redemption most complete and glorious, and raise them to the greatest height of felicity and glory.

It is now to be more particularly considered and shewn, How the everlasting punishment of the wicked is suited, and even necessary, to answer these ends.

It has been already observed and shewn, how well suited, and necessary, endless punishment is to make a full and most glorious display of the divine character, in the view of the blessed. In this will be seen, as could not be seen, so clearly and to such advantage, by any other medium, or without this, the infinite greatness, power and terrible majesty of JEHOVAH: And also his infinite excellence and worthiness, and his hatred and displeasure, his indignation and wrath, against sin; and his infinite benevolence and goodness, to which sin is opposed. The smoke of their torment shall ascend up in the sight of the blessed forever and ever, and serve, as a most clear glass, always before their eyes, to give them a constant, bright and most affecting view of all these. And all this display of the Divine character and glory will be in favor of the redeemed, and most entertaining, and give the highest pleasure to all who love God, and raise their happiness to ineffable heights, whose felicity consists primarily in the knowledge and enjoyment of God. This eternal punishment must therefore be unspeakably to their advantage; and will add such immense

mense degrees of glory and happiness to the kingdom of God, as inconceivably to overbalance all they will suffer, who shall fall under this righteous punishment, and render it all, in this view and connexion, an infinite good. But it will further appear, how useful and necessary the endless punishment of the wicked is, to the highest good and happiness of the redeemed, and all the friends of God, by attending to the following particulars.

1. The eternal existence of sin, in all its horrors, acted out without restraint, with the infinite evil which is the natural and just consequence of it, taking place in the sight of the inhabitants of heaven, will serve to manifest and illustrate the beauty, excellence and worth of holiness, and the happiness of all holy beings; and forever brighten the character of God and all his friends, and render the blessed unspeakably more sensible of their happiness, and of the beauty and happiness of each other, than they could be, if there were no such contrast.

It is well known, that contraries illustrate each other; and that the greatest beauty cannot appear to the best advantage, without a *shade*: That deformity gives a lustre to beauty; and evil magnifies and sweetens the contrary good. This contrast will take place to the highest possible degree, and to the greatest advantage, forever, by endless punishment, and can not be without it: Therefore it is necessary to the highest happiness and glory of heaven.

2. The eternal punishment of the wicked, in the sight of the redeemed, will serve, incessantly, to keep fresh in their view the infinite evil of sin; and, in the most effectual, lively manner, teach them, and make them *feel* their own infinite ill desert, and the infinitely evil case in which they should have been, had God treated them according to their deserts: And so keep in clear and constant view the infinite guilt and misery, from which they

they have been redeemed; and maintain in their minds a lively growing sense of all this. There are many other ways, in which they are, and will be, taught these things; but this will add great instruction, which they could not have without it; and it is better suited, than any other, to keep up their attention, and give them a more lively, constant, affecting apprehension and sense of them. It is of great importance, and necessary, that the redeemed should be under the best advantage to see these truths; in order to their glorifying God, in the best manner, and enjoying the highest happiness. For,

3. This is necessary, in order to their most clearly seeing, and celebrating, to the highest degree, the goodness of God, his astonishing grace and mercy in their redemption. Had there been no sin, guilt and misery, there could have been no such thing as redeeming love and grace, ever known, or thought of, by creatures: And this is great in proportion to the greatness of the guilt, vileness, ill desert, and misery of the sinner; and the former cannot be known, any further than the latter are discovered and seen: Therefore, redeeming love and goodness can be no further seen and celebrated, by the redeemed, than they realize their ill desert, and the infinite guilt and misery from which they are redeemed: In the light of this only is seen the goodness and sovereign grace of God to them, in their redemption: And in proportion to their sight and sense of this, will they feel and adore the goodness of God to the redeemed; and their hearts glow with the most sincere, sweet gratitude and joy, while they give all the praise and glory to God, for the distinction made between them, and those who, in their sight, are forever unutterably miserable; and their enjoyment and happiness, their love, gratitude and praise, will rise in proportion to their view and sense of God's infinite, astonishing goodness and de-

stinguishing

stinguishing, sovereign grace to them, and all the redeemed. Therefore, while they behold the damned, in all their sin and awful misery, and doomed thus to suffer without end, and this will be full in their sight, it will be the occasion of their rising proportionably high, in their exercises of love and praise, and in the sweetest sense of redeeming love and grace: And in them will be most completely fulfilled the last words of the prophet Isaiah: " And it shall come to pass, that from one new moon to another, and from one sabbath to another, shall all flesh come to worship before me, saith the Lord. And they shall go forth, and look upon the men that have transgressed against me: For their worm shall not die, neither shall their fire be quenched; and they shall be an abhorring to all flesh." The inhabitants of heaven, while they are worshipping God, shall have in full view the men that for their transgressions are cast into endless burnings; and this sight will give them most clear and affecting apprehensions of the infinite evil of sin, and the just desert of it; and in this light they will abhor sin and the sinners; approve of God's righteous judgments; and see and adore the infinite goodness and astonishing grace, by which they are redeemed from this infinite depth of sin and misery; which will animate them in all their worship and praises, and unspeakably add to their increasing felicity.

The apostle Paul sets the punishment of the wicked exactly in this light, Rom. ix 22 23. "What if God, willing *to shew his wrath, and make his power known, endured with much long suffering the vessels of wrath, fitted to destruction: And that he might make known the riches of his glory on the vessels of mercy, which he had before prepared unto glory?"* Here one end of God's shewing his wrath, and making his power known, in the eternal punishment of the wicked, is represented to

be,

be, that he might make known the riches of his glory on the vessels of mercy: That is, that he might, by this means make known to the redeemed, the riches of his glorious grace, exercised towards them in their salvation.

4. The endless punishment of the wicked being always in the sight of the redeemed, will serve to manifest to them, as nothing else can, and keep constantly in their view, the power, dignity, worthiness, love and grace of the Redeemer, who was able and willing to redeem them from such a state of sin and punishment, of infinite guilt and wretchedness: Or, it will make a bright and eternal display of the glorious character and infinite worth of the Mediator.

They who suppose it would not be just to punish sinners with everlasting destruction, or that it is inconsistent with the goodness of God to punish them forever, make redemption a very small and inconsiderable matter. It is really, according to this, redemption from little or no evil. As it was nothing very great, to make atonement for sins which did not deserve infinite evil; and which could not be punished with everlasting destruction, consistent with the goodness of God; and which his goodness obliged him to pardon, and so make the sinner happy, had there been no Redeemer. For men cannot be redeemed from evil, which they do not deserve; or which cannot be inflicted on them, consistent with the goodness of God. This sinks and hides the character of a Redeemer, and at once reduces redemption to very little or nothing. The actual existence of eternal punishment, in the sight of all intelligent creatures, will serve to confute these unworthy notions of God and of redemption; and is necessary in order to do it most effectually, and to set the Redeemer in an infinitely more important and glorious light forever. His infinite greatness

greatness and worth, the value and preciousness of his blood appear, in that, by his sufferings and obedience unto death, he could atone for *such sins*, and deliver from *such punishment*; and merit and procure pardon and favor for such infinitely guilty, ill deserving creatures. And the almighty power, and wonderful condescention, love and grace of Christ, will appear in a most affecting light, in his being able and willing to pluck such vile, obstinate sinners from those everlasting burnings; and will, by this punishment, be kept in fresh remembrance, and cause his glorious character and works to be more and more known and celebrated forever.

And all this will be in favor of the redeemed, and will add unspeakably to their happiness; for the more glorious Christ appears to them, the more his dignity and worth come into their view, and the greater their redemption appears to be, and the clearer sight they have of the love and grace of the Redeemer, and the more indebted and obliged they are to him, and the higher he is exalted in their salvation ; *so much the more happy they must be ;* and with proportionably greater sweetness and joy will they forever sing, " Worthy is the Lamb that was slain, and has redeemed us to God by his blood, to receive power, and riches, and wisdom, and strength, and honor, and glory, and blessing, forever and ever."

UPON THE WHOLE, it appears, from the view we have had of this subject, so far from being inconsistent with the goodness of God to punish sinners forever, that the ends of divine goodness are answered by this to the highest possible degree, and as they could not be without it, or in any other possible way ; so that it is utterly inconsistent with infinite goodness, not to punish them thus. This eternal punishment reflects such light on the Divine character, government and works, especially the

work

work of redemption; and makes such a bright display of the worthiness and grandeur of the Redeemer, and of divine love and grace to the redeemed; and is the occasion of so much happiness in heaven; and so necessary, in order to the highest glory, and greatest increasing felicity of God's everlasting kingdom; that, should it cease, and this fire could be extinguished, it would, in a great measure, obscure the light of heaven, and put an end to great part of the happiness and glory of the blessed, and be an irreparable detriment to God's eternal kingdom; most contrary to infinite wisdom and goodness. And however great an evil the endless misery of so many millions is, in itself considered; yet, it being not only just, but the necessary means of such infinite glory and happiness to the kingdom of God; in this view, and in comparison with this, it sinks into nothing, and is wholly absorbed, as to the evil of it, and lost, in the unspeakable glory and felicity, of which it is the occasion; and is, on the whole, most desirable, and really becomes, in this connexion, an important good, essential to the perfection of the Divine government, and the highest glory and happiness of God's eternal kingdom. How inconsiderate and unreasonable then, must they be, who disbelieve the doctrine of endless punishment, and oppose it, as inconsistent with infinite goodness. *

SECTION

---

* Some have argued from the aversion of a tender parent or fond mother to the pain and sufferings of their children, by being cast into the fire, &c. and from the desire that men profess to have, that all men should be saved; that these have more goodness, than *they* ascribe to God, who believe he will cast multitudes of his creatures into everlasting burnings; and hence infer, that endless punishment is inconsistent with infinite goodness.

SECTION V.

CONTAINING a Number of Questions and Answers, relating to the Doctrine of endless Punishment.

UPON the subject, as it has been now stated, the following queries may arise in the minds of some, which ought to be answered: And thereby the truth may be made more clear, and further confirmed.

I.

If there were any weight or propriety in this way of arguing, it proves that God never did, nor ever will inflict *any evil* on his creatures; as much as it does, that he will not punish them forever. It proves, for instance, that he did not rain fire and brimstone on the inhabitants of Sodom, and cause them, both old and young, to welter in the keenest anguish, till they expired: And that he does not inflict those excruciating pains and tortures on children, and others, which tender parents and friends often behold with the utmost aversion, distress and anguish. And since this way of arguing is as much against *known facts*, as it is against endless punishment, it is certainly just as consistent with the existence of the latter, as of the former; and therefore is not worthy of the least regard. And when any one pretends to argue in this way, he discovers himself to be a very shallow reasoner, or a stranger to uprightness and honesty. Had Abraham reason to think he had more goodness than his Maker, because he was shocked at the proposal of destroying the inhabitants of Sodom, and interceded for them?

When parents in Israel had a disobedient son, they were commanded to bring him forth into public, and witness against him, that he might be stoned to death. Deut. xxi. 18,—21. If the parents love and tenderness towards their children, led them to refuse to execute this law, or to look upon it hard and cruel, and reluct at the thought of having one of their children put to death in this manner; had they reason to think the God of Israel severe and cruel, or that he had less goodness than themselves?

A benevolent man may wish and pray for the salvation of all

I. Though it be granted, that the blessed will receive great advantage by the eternal destruction of such vast numbers of the human race, and there will be unspeakably more happiness in the kingdom of God, than could be, were there no such punishment; yet, how can it be consistent with goodness, or even impartial justice, to make part of the human race happy, at the expense of the rest, and by means of their eternal misery? Would it not be much better for *all* to be free from misery, and have a less and moderate share of happiness; than for some to be so very miserable forever, as the means of the greater happiness of others? And would not this be more agreeable to a benevolent, generous mind? Would it not much rather chuse to have a less share of happiness; than to enjoy more, at such amazing expense and cost of his fellow-creatures, even their everlasting misery.

Ans.

All those whom he sees, or that do exist in the world, as their salvation is, in itself considered, desirable, and he knows not that this is inconsistent with the general good: But if any one, or a number, should be pointed out to him, who deserve to perish, and he should know that this was necessary for the glory of God, and the good of his kingdom; he would not ask nor desire that they should be saved; unless his benevolence were very imperfect. When a king or judge condemns a criminal to death, and sees the sentence executed, because it is necessary for the public good; is not this an act of goodness? Or shall we think the tender mother, wife, or child of the criminal, who wishes, and, in agonies of pity, implores his pardon and reprieve, and cannot bear the thought of his execution; to have and shew more benevolence and goodness, than the king or judge? And if these shou'd boast of their benevolence, and represent the wise and good judge as inexorably cruel; they would appear to the friends of good government, and the public good, just as do the advocates for *universal salvation*, when they boast of this as the Benevolent plan, and represent the opposers of it a uncharitable, inhumane and cruel.

Anf. 1. Since they who shall be miserable forever, do deserve this punishment; neither they, nor any other creature, will have any reason to complain, because they are thus punished. And if God can, by executing justice on them, answer great and important ends to himself, his government and kingdom, which could not be obtained, but must be forever lost, without it; and can render his kingdom unspeakably more happy and glorious, than it could otherwise be; surely all true friends to God and his kingdom, who desire and seek the greatest good of the whole, must be pleased, and greatly rejoice in it. This leads to

Anf. 2. Since the good of which endless punishment will be the means, will be so vastly great, as immensely to overbalance the evil; so that it will be as nothing compared with the good, every degree of evil producing millions of millions of degrees of good and happiness; and there would be, on the whole, infinitely less good, should this punishment cease; it must be the dictate and choice of infinite benevolence, thus to punish. And that must be a very partial, imperfect, defective goodness, which, in this case, would give up the greatest general good, for the sake of an infinitely less good to some unworthy individuals: Such a disposition is not true benevolence, but the contrary. This has been observed before, and it is presumed is evident, beyond all possible doubt. Therefore,

Anf. 3. The generous, benevolent mind, which desires and seeks the greatest good of the whole, the glory of God, and the greatest glory and happiness of his kingdom, must chuse, and be pleased with that just, eternal misery of the wicked, which is so necessary to promote this, to the highest degree: And the greater and more generous and benevolent the mind is, the more pleasure will it take in such a plan. And he only, whose

whose heart is contracted, partial and selfish, and, consequently, an enemy to the greatest general good, will object and oppose it.

All will allow, there may be wisdom and goodness in subjecting a person to a great degree of deserved evil, in order to promote his unspeakably greater good; so that the evil he suffers, becomes the means of his immensely greater happiness forever; and that this is vastly preferable to no suffering and misery. In this case, therefore, the misery suffered is, on the whole, a good; it being the necessary means of making him unspeakably more happy, than he could have been, had he not suffered. For that which is the necessary means of so much good, though *in itself* undesirable and evil, is, in this connexion, a real good.

This may serve to illustrate the case before us. Here indeed, the person who suffers does not enjoy the good of which his sufferings are the means; but the happy part of the community. Nevertheless, when we consider, that they who are miserable, suffer justly, and this becomes the means of infinitely greater good to the whole; we must be sensible, that, as in the case proposed, suffering is much preferable to no suffering, and, on the whole, becomes a great good; it must be so in the case under consideration. For the evil is, in itself, no greater, from those particular persons suffering, and not others; and the good, of which those sufferings are the means, is as great and desirable, as if they who enjoy it had themselves been the subjects of the sufferings, were this possible.

II. It may be queried, Whether it be not undesirable, and must not be considered as an unhappiness, that all this good cannot take place without any suffering? Would not this be infinitely better, and more agreeable, if it were possible? And surely this is possible with God.

Sect. V.

If it be not; must not this be crossing, and the source of uneasiness and regret to the infinitely good Being, and to all his benevolent friends?

Ans. 1. It is certain, that God hath taken this method to promote the highest good of the universe; by ordering things so, that a great degree of sin and suffering should exist, in order to it. Infinite benevolence seeks the greatest good of the whole; therefore, if this could be effected as well, and to as great a degree, without any sin or suffering, God would have prevented the existence of these: Consequently, all this sin and misery do take place, because they are necessary to the greatest good of the whole; so that it could not be obtained in any other way.

All must allow, that God will answer some good end by all the sin and misery in the world, which could not be so well answered without them; or confess, that his government and administrations are imperfect and unwise. And if the evil that has actually taken place is designed, and necessary, to answer the most important and best end; then it may be as necessary, for the same reason, that it should continue forever, to answer the same end, to the highest degree. And that it is so, and the reason of it, has been shewn above. This, therefore, being a known fact, cannot be disputed. And we may hence safely conclude there is nothing undesirable and disagreeable in it; yea, we are certain there is not, if it be desirable, that the greatest good of the whole should take place.

Ans. 2. Infinite power is not an ability to effect impossibles, or to make contradictions consistent: For not to be able to do this, is no defect of power, as these are not the objects of power, any more than sound is the object of sight. And there is nothing disagreeable in this; but on the contrary, it would be undesirable there should be any such power, were it possible. It

It is impossible that a creature should be made capable of enjoying an infinite degree of happiness, in a limited duration; just as impossible as it is that he should be a God. Nor can creatures be happy, unless some method be taken, and means used, to make them so. Should any one ask, Why every creature is not made to enjoy as great a degree of happiness as his Creator? And why there are not millions of creatures more than there are, or ever will be? (For God cannot create so many, that this question may not be asked, Why did he not create more?) And why they might not all be thus happy, without any way being taken, or means used to make them so? And whether it will not be eternally considered as an unhappiness, and matter of grief and regret, that all this cannot be? He may be answered, That all these are in their own nature absolutely impossible, as they imply a contradiction; and therefore not desirable; but the contrary. For what is impossible, and implies a contradiction, is not desirable: And therefore this can give no uneasiness to a perfect mind.

And is not this a sufficient and satisfactory answer to the query proposed? A Being of infinite power, wisdom and goodness, can be under no restraint; and the highest possible good of the universe will be effected, by ways and means that are most wise and best. This is all that a perfectly good mind can wish and desire. And therefore, there can be no possible ground of the least uneasiness to such a mind; but every thing is perfectly suited to give it all the enjoyment and happiness that can be desired.

III. If it be granted, that endless punishment were necessary, and would answer all the good ends which have been mentioned, had there been no Mediator and Redeemer; yet, since the Son of God has, in the human

man nature, suffered the curse, even that which, considering his infinite greatness and dignity, is equivalent to the eternal sufferings of men; so that God may be just, and maintain and honor his own character, law and government, in pardoning and granting complete salvation to sinners, for Christ's sake: And in his sufferings may be seen clearly displayed, all those things that have been mentioned, as manifested in the endless punishment of sinners: And since the merits of Christ are as sufficient for the salvation of *all*, as of only a part of the human race: Since all this is true, it is queried, Why it is necessary, or proper, that any of mankind should suffer eternal punishment? Are not all the ends of suffering answered, in the sufferings of Christ? What need then is there of endless punishment?

Answer. It is granted, that the mediation and sufferings of Christ, have so far answered the law, and the end of the punishment therein denounced against sin, that God may, consistent with his character and law, pardon and save every one of the human race, who believes in Christ, being heartily pleased with his mediatorial character and works; as by his sufferings for sinners, the same, and as much regard and honor is paid to the divine character, law and government, as if they had suffered forever: And hereby are manifested the infinite evil of sin, and the infinite ill desert and misery of the sinner; and the wonderful love and grace of God, &c. And therefore, in this view and sense, what Christ hath done and suffered for man, is as sufficient for the salvation of any one, as of another, and for *all*, as for part of the human race.

Nevertheless, this does not lay God under the least obligation actually to save all: And it still remains for his infinite wisdom and goodness to determine this; whether all shall be saved, or only part of mankind:

And

And if but part, how great a part, and what individuals shall be included in that number; so as shall in the best manner, and highest degree, answer the ends of redemption, and promote the greatest good of the whole.

And though the sufferings of Christ do lay a sufficient foundation for the salvation of sinners, and make a bright and glorious display of those truths which have been mentioned, relating to the divine perfections, law, sin, &c. yet, the eternal sufferings of some of the human race may be necessary, to make and continue a manifestation of these things, to the best advantage, and so as to promote the greatest happiness of the blessed; yea, in all respects, as necessary, as if Christ had not suffered, necessary, in order to complete, or fully accomplish the ends of Christ's sufferings; so that redemption by Christ would, without this, be very imperfect; as all the ends of divine wisdom and goodness could not be answered, if all were saved. And that this is really so, is abundantly evident, from what has been said concerning the ends that will be answered by eternal punishment, in the preceding section. *

The sufferings of Christ are a peculiar and striking manifestation of the sacredness of the divine law, God's hatred of sin, and the infinite evil and malignity of it, &c. A manifestation, which could not have been so fully made, had not Christ suffered as he did. Nevertheless, the eternal sufferings of sinners are suited, in many respects, to instruct and affect creatures, as the sufferings of Christ alone could not; and the former are necessary to be joined with the latter, that the display and instruction may be most full and complete. The sufferings of Christ were temporary, and soon over; and though they will never be forgotten, yet they cannot be so clearly in view, as the present, constant, endless sufferings

* See page 151, 152, 153, 154.

ferings of the wicked; and the latter will be the means of keeping up a more clear and fresh view of the former, than otherwise could be: And, at the same time, will be a constant, eternal exhibition before their eyes, of the infinite odiousness and misery of the sinner, when sin has its natural and deserved course and issue; which is so necessary, in order to a proper, full and most affecting view of the power and worthiness of Christ; the efficacy of his mediation; the greatness of the salvation by him, and his infinite love and grace in dying to save sinners, &c. which has been particularly considered above.

It hence appears, that the sufferings of Christ for sinners, and the abundant sufficiency of his merit for their salvation, render eternal punishment not the less necessary, but, in all respects, more so; and unspeakably more important and useful, as it is necessary to make this salvation most complete and glorious, and answers more important ends, than it could, had there been no salvation for sinners by a Mediator.

But this may be further illustrated by the following particulars:

1. If all the human race were saved, it never could be seen, as now it will be, how exceeding perverse and obstinate men are, in their sins. In the eternal destruction of men, this will be set in the most clear and convincing light. God is using the greatest variety of means, with men of different ages, nations, and capacities, and in different and various circumstances, suited, in the best manner, to influence them, and bring them to repentance; urging them by infinitely weighty arguments and motives, to embrace the offered Saviour (which, by the way, could not be, in any measure, so strong and urgent, were there no eternal destruction, for the disobedient) and yet, in opposition to all these, they

refuse

refuse the offered salvation; abuse and trample upon divine love and mercy, and the Saviour himself, and madly rush on to eternal perdition. This will make a most bright and endless discovery of the infatuation, madness and malignity of sin, and the obstinacy and vileness of the sinner; which must have remained in a great measure out of sight, and never could have been so fully known, and realized by the saved, were there no awful instances of this, who shall suffer the consequences of it forever. If all did believe on Christ, and accept of the offered salvation, it never could have been so fully known, that men were obstinate and vile enough, to slight this salvation, and trample on Christ, under the greatest light and advantages; and perseveringly choose eternal destruction, rather than submit to the Saviour.

It is of the greatest importance, that this should be seen forever; that the redeemed may have a constant and increasing sense of the nature of sin, and know how far they were from salvation, notwithstanding all possible means and advantages; and realize the infinite power and grace of Christ, in their recovery; that they may give the glory to God, which is due to him, and enjoy redeeming love and grace, in it's full extent, sweetness and glory.

2. If all were saved, the real need, and absolute necessity, of an atonement for sin, in order to the salvation of men, would not appear in so clear a light, as it will do, in the eternal punishment of the impenitent. If all were saved, they would be in some degree sensible of the need of this atonement: But it would not appear so clear and certain, that there is no other possible way of salvation; and that all must have been miserable forever, had it not been for the atonement and redemption of Christ; as it now will, when all that light and rej ct
the s

this atonement, through this life, actually perish forever, without any possible remedy.

3. If all mankind were saved, the *sovereignty* of divine grace, in the salvation of men, would not be so manifest, as it now will be.

Indeed, grace or mere favor, is in it's own nature sovereign grace; that is, it is exercised towards those who have not the least claim, or desert of it. And the further a creature is from any desert of the favor granted; and the more unworthy and ill deserving he is, and the more he has done to provoke displeasure and wrath, the more sovereign is the grace. And therefore, the more the creature's ill desert *appears*, the more the favor granted *appears* to be mere sovereign grace; and the greater manifestation there is of the riches and glory of this.

But this will be made to appear, in the strongest light, to the redeemed, when they behold those in everlasting misery, as their just and deserved portion, who are no more ill deserving than themselves; and know that mere sovereign grace hath made the distinction; since, had it not been for this grace, they themselves would infallibly have run on to destruction, and been as sinful and miserable, as those who are actually lost; notwithstanding the offers of salvation made to them, and the means and advantages they enjoyed. Nothing can be better suited to keep this in the clearest view forever, than this *actual distinction*, made by divine grace, in saving some, while others are given over to deserved, everlasting destruction. And without this, or were all saved, the manifestation of this, would have been comparatively dark, and very imperfect.

From this view of the matter, it appears easy to see how important and necessary it is, that all should not be saved, in order that the Redeemer and redemption, might

might appear in their true greatness and splendor; and the highest manifestation of glorious, sovereign grace be made in the salvation of sinners; and the greatest happiness of the saved promoted: Though, at the same time, it is not pretended, that any are able to discern *all the ends*, that divine wisdom and goodness will answer, by this dispensation.

IV. If it be granted, that it is necessary, in order to render the work of redemption most complete and glorious, and the redeemed happy to the highest degree, that all should not be saved: Yet, it is queried, Why there should be *so few* saved; and almost all mankind lost, notwithstanding all that has been done for the salvation of men? Surely it cannot be for the greatest good of the whole, to have the most of mankind destroyed, and but few have the benefit of redemption.

Ans. 1. No man is in any measure able to determine what number, or what proportion of the whole, must be saved or lost, in order to answer the most important ends; the ends that have been mentioned to be obtained by endless punishment, and many more which are now out of our sight. If we knew the exact proportion between the saved and the lost; and that the former were few, compared with the latter; this would be no more a ground of objection against the doctrine of endless punishment, than if the proportion was directly the other way. And to suppose, that the less the number of those that shall be punished is, so much the better, seems to be giving up the doctrine of endless punishment; and to suppose it would be, on the whole, best to have none lost. Though *we* are utterly incompetent judges in this matter, infinite wisdom can determine it, without the possibility of a mistake. God knows what proportion of the human race, even the exact number, and what individuals, may be saved, consistent with the

greatest

greatest good of the whole; and how many must be punished forever, in order to answer the best and most important ends. And all have reason to acquiesce in his disposal; and to rejoice that it will be determined by infinite wisdom and goodness. And all wi*l* rejoice in this, who are friends to righteousness, wisdom, and benevolence; that is, friends to God, and his uncontrollable dominion. Man has no right or ability to judge what is best, in this case; or what will in fact be the issue, any further than God hath revealed it in his word.

Anſ. 2. We have no reason to conclude, from the word of God, that but few, or a very small part of mankind will be saved: But, from *that*, there is reason to believe, that many more of the human race will be happy, than miserable.

It has indeed been believed by many, that the number of the redeemed will be very small, compared with those who will perish; partly from several passages of scripture; and partly from what has taken place in the world hitherto; as the church of Christ has been comparatively very small, and but few have appeared to walk in the narrow way which leadeth unto life. But when those scriptures, and this fact, are carefully examined, and compared with other parts of scripture, it will doubtless appear, that no such thing can be inferred; but the contrary.

Our Saviour says, "Strait is the gate, and narrow is the way which leadeth unto life, and *few* there be that find it." And, "Many are called, but *few* chosen." And he calls his disciples a *little flock*. Christ in these words speaks of the then present time, and of what took place, at that time; and does not say, that but few of mankind, compared with the whole, shall ever find the way to life, and be chosen to salvation; or that his church shall always be a little flock: But he has said

the

the contrary. He represents his church by a "Grain of mustard seed, which a man took and sowed in his field; which indeed is the least of all seeds; but when it is grown, it is the greatest among herbs, and becometh a tree; so that the birds of the air come and lodge in the branches thereof." And he likens it " Unto leaven, which a woman took and hid in three measures of meal, till the whole was leavened." Denoting, that though it was small in its beginning, it should increase and become great, and fill the world. And the same thing is represented in Daniel, by a stone cut out of the mountain without hands, which became a great mountain, and *filled the whole earth*. And the same is expressed in the following words; " And the kingdom and dominion, and the greatness of the kingdom under the whole heaven, shall be given to the people of the saints of the Most High. The kingdoms of this world are become the kingdoms of our Lord, and of his Christ." According to this, the time is coming when all nations shall be the servants of Christ, and the world shall be full of his people; agreeable to many other prophecies of the same thing, too many to be recited here. "And it shall come to pass *in the last days*, that the mountain of the Lord's house shall be established in the top of the mountains, and shall be exalted above the hills; and *all nations shall flow unto it*. For the earth shall be full of the knowledge of the Lord, as the waters cover the sea."

They who have attended well to the Bible must be sensible, that the time is yet to come in which salvation by Christ shall take place, as it never has yet done: His church shall flourish and fill the world; and Satan's kingdom be utterly destroyed in the earth. And this happy and glorious day of salvation shall continue *a thousand years*. In this thousand years of peace, and prosperity

Sect. V.

prosperity, when the people shall be *all righteous*, mankind will naturally propagate and multiply, as they never yet have done, and fill the whole face of the earth; so that there will be many thousand times more living in the world at one time, than there ever yet have been. It is easy to shew, that in such a state, many more people will exist in a thousand years, than have existed before; yea, many thousands to one; supposing this thousand years shall be the seventh thousand years of the world; which supposition is agreeable to scripture. If the greater part that live in the preceding six thousand years, do perish; yet if all, or most, who shall exist in the seventh thousand years, shall be saved, there will, on the whole, be many more of mankind saved, than lost; yea, it may be, many thousands to one. But as this does not so immediately affect the subject we are considering, it is needless to enlarge upon it here.

THE reader has now the doctrine of endless punishment laid before him, as it is revealed, and abundantly asserted in the word of God: And the justice of this punishment, and necessity of it, in order to answer the most important purposes; to render the work of redemption most complete and glorious, and promote the highest good and happiness of the universe; so that it is a real good, and necessary part of the most wise and benevolent plan; and therefore most pleasing to infinite goodness, and best suited to excite the joy and praise of every benevolent mind.*

---

* And in this light may be seen the absurdity of that enthusiastic harangue of Mr. *Jeremiah White*, who lived in the last century, lately published in Boston [see *Salvation for all men*. p. 1, 2, 3, 4.] which may well be considered as the very dregs of the enthusiasm, and religious frenzy, which took place, to so great a degree, in his day. He was himself so pleased and charmed with his scheme of *universal salvation*,

that

that in a conceit of his own superior benevolence he caressed himself with fanatic complacence and joy; and then exclaims, "He is not a christian, he is not a man, he hath cut off the tenderness and bowels of a man, he hath lost humanity itself, he hath not so much charity as Dives expressed in hell, that cannot cry out, THIS IS GOOD NEWS IF IT BE TRUE!"

As Mr. White cannot now answer for himself; his voucher, who introduces this as an instance of the author's ingenuity, piety and benevolence; and all the advocates for temporary future punishment, in opposition to endless. may be desired to answer and clear up the following difficulties, which seem to attend their scheme.

If he who has any benevolence, will be pleased with the news, that there is no such thing as endless punishment; will he not be glad to hear, that there is no future punishment at all? And will he not be sorry, that there ever have been, & still are, so much sin and misery in the world; and must not this be matter of grief to him to all eternity, whenever he thinks of it? And why must not the infinitely Benevolent Mind be in the same way affected with this, to an infinitely greater degree?

According to this, it would be much best, and most pleasing to the benevolent, to have no such thing as sin or misery in the universe. Why then is there any such thing? How can it be accounted for, that they should take place, under the all-perfect government of an infinitely benevolent Being?

If it be said, These have taken place under God's government, when he was able to have prevented their existence, in order to answer some good and important ends, which could not be accomplished without them; so that it is, on the whole, best they should exist, as they have done; and will issue in the greatest general good: It will be then asked, If such a degree of sin and misery as has taken place, and will take place to the end of the world, and after the day of judgment, in a long, though temporary punishment, be necessary to promote the highest general good; why may not endless punishment be as necessary, and more so, to promote the highest possible general good? Who is able to say, who dare say, it is not? If any presume to do it, let them answer what has been said above, to prove the contrary: And, which is of more importance, let them shew that it is not declared in

sacred

sacred writ: Or let them answer it to their Maker at the last day.

It is further and more particularly asked, Why there will be *any* future punishment? What end will this great temporary evil answer?

If it be answered, That this is necessary in order to reclaim, and bring to repentance, those who in this life were obstinate, and persevered in rebellion: It is still asked, Why God does not, by the power of his spirit and grace, bring all to repentance and conversion in this life? He does it in some instances; and he is equally able to do it in *every* instance, and bring *all* to close with Christ in this world: Why then does he not do it, and effectually prevent all that dreadful scene of sin and misery, which must take place in a long punishment? Such a punishment has no more tendency to bring them to repentance, than the means used with them in this world; yea, it may be made evident, it hath not so much, if any. And it is certain no means will effect it, without divine influence; and God must, by this, convert them, after all, and save them by the washing of regeneration, and the renewing of the Holy Ghost. Why then is not this always done in this life, if done at all; and all future punishment prevented?

If it be said, This future, temporary punishment is necessary for God to shew his wrath against sin, and his justice in punishing the sinner according to his desert: And as he can deserve only a temporary punishment; when he has suffered that, he will be delivered. Mr. White says something like this, when he speaks of "All the methods which God uses in his holy and glorious wisdom and prudence, *in giving way to the entrance of sin,* and then *inflaming the anguish of it by the law,* that he may thereby have occasion *to glorify his wrath against it, and his justice;* and so make his way *to the more glorious illustration of his grace and love in the close.*" This excites the following observations and questions.

1. If sin deserves an endless punishment, then in order to God's shewing his displeasure, so as "to glorify his wrath against it, and his justice," he must inflict such a punishment. To inflict an infinitely less punishment than the sinner deserves, will be so far from glorifying the wrath and justice of God; that it will make a contrary appearance, and look as if

if God hated sin infinitely less than he does; and that sin does not deserve endless punishment; and that justice is satisfied with something infinitely short of it. How then can God glorify his wrath against sin, and his justice, in punishing it; unless he inflict an endless punishment?

If the subject of a king should blaspheme him, and seek to ruin his whole kingdom; and the king should punish him, only by laying a fine on him of *one penny*; would not the language of this be, that he looked on his character and kingdom to be worth no more than one penny; and that in this punishment was a proper expression of his wrath against the criminal, and a glorious exercise of justice; this being all he deserved? Would this be *glory*, or *disgrace*?

Let it be *proved* then, that no sinner can *deserve* endless punishment, before any thing is said of God's glorifying his wrath and justice, by a temporary punishment.

2. If sin deserves only a temporary punishment, then, when the sinner has suffered this, even as much as he deserves, justice is fully satisfied, and he has no more ill desert, and must, in *justice*, be delivered. How then does his deliverance and salvation make a " more glorious illustration of God's *grace and love*, in the close," than if the creature had never sinned, and had not been punished? Yea, Is there *any* grace and mercy manifested in this? Surely no. For grace and mercy is favor shewed to the ill deserving; and not doing what justice requires. And if the sinner has suffered all the punishment he deserved, so that his guilt and ill desert is entirely done away, and he has no more of it than Adam had, when he was first created; what need has he of the atonement of Christ, and salvation by him, any more than Adam had before he sinned? What need then was there of Christ, in order to the salvation of all men; and what hand or glory will he have in the deliverance and salvation of those who have suffered all they deserve for their sins?

These questions and observations arise from it's being allowed and said, in order to account for the sin and misery that have actually taken place, That God could have prevented their existence, but did not, because they are necessary to answer good and important ends. This is allowed by Mr. White, and many others, who deny the endless duration of future punishment.

But

Sect. V.

But there are others, who take another method to account for the introduction of sin and consequent misery, and their continuance in the world; and to make this consistent with divine goodness, while they deny that endless punishment is consistent with it; they say, God could not prevent sin and consequent misery, consistent with the moral agency and freedom of man; and therefore, in consequence of creatures being made and continued free agents, sin was introduced. And as the methods taken to reclaim men in this life are, in many instances, ineffectual; they will be punished in the future state, till they submit, and obtain deliverance.

This notion is so inconsistent with the bible, and contrary to all reason, that it is difficult to conceive, how any man who has the use of these, should embrace it, and rest satisfied. The scriptures represent God as supreme, and infinitely above control, doing what he pleases in heaven and on earth; and having the hearts of men in his hands, directing and turning them as he pleases; even turning them from sin to holiness, and working in them to will and to do, &c. And that God does all this, consistent with their freedom and accountableness for all their moral exercises and conduct. And what reasonable man would chuse to have a God, who is at the control and beck of his creatures, not able to give them their rights, and maintain his own supremacy; so that he is obliged, in a great degree, to give up his dominion into their hands, and suffer them to introduce that, which he would with all his heart prevent, were he able!

But not to dwell on this, which is not directly to the present purpose; it is now to be inquired, Whether this scheme is in any degree favorable to the doctrine of the salvation of all men.

If God could not prevent sin consistently with the freedom of man, how can he recover men from sin, when they have once fallen under the dominion of it, and not infringe on their freedom? If he could not keep sin out of the world, what evidence is there, that he can clear the world of it, and put an end to the rebellion, after it has had such a mighty spread, and continued so long? Is it not probable; yea, even certain, that it will continue forever, notwithstanding any thing he can do? Therefore, if it be certain that God

does

does all he can to bring all men to holiness and happiness; what evidence is there, that this will ever be effected? If all the means used with men, in this world, be not sufficient to bring them to repentance, and 'tis supposed God uses the best means, and takes the best and most likely methods, and does all he can, to effect it; what evidence is there that he will ever be able to recover all men from sin, by any means whatsoever? Is it certain, is it probable, that any degree or length of future punishment will be sufficient to effect this, since all other more likely means fail? This cannot be. And if it was *certain*, that future punishment would bring all men to repentance; what security can there be, that they will not relapse into sin, and oblige their Maker to continue their punishment; and what end can their be of this, so long as God cannot prevent sin, consistent with the freedom of his creatures? There can be no possible security against sin, and punishment without end, on this plan, unless God should annihilate all the moral agents he has made, and so put an eternal end to his moral government! Is not this a poor, miserable foundation, upon which to build an assurance of the eternal happiness of all men?

Let the advocates for the salvation of all men give a fair and satisfactory answer to all these questions, and to what has been produced against this doctrine in the foregoing sheets; and remove all these difficulties from their scheme. Or, if they cannot do this, let them give up their dangerous notion, and admit the belief of endless punishment, and that scheme of divine truth, so consistent with the word of God, and so plainly and abundantly inculcated there; which reflects such glory on the Divine character and gives a rational, satisfactory account of the introduction of sin and misery, under the most wise and happy government of JEHOVAH; and the continuance of them forever, for the greatest good of the whole; and against which, there can be no reasonable objection.

SECTION

SECTION VI.

CONTAINING Inferences from the Doctrine of endless Punishment, and a practical Improvement of it.

I. THE doctrine of endless punishment being thus established from the holy scriptures, and vindicated and supported by reason; it follows, that all those doctrines, and that experimental or practical religion, which are inconsistent with this doctrine, are false and delusive.

If we were able to take a thorough, comprehensive view of the subject, and examine it without any prejudice and darkness; it would doubtless be found, that no false scheme of religion, in doctrine or practice, can stand this test, and be reconciled, in all its parts, to *this doctrine*; but that all such schemes do clash with it; however ignorant of it they may be who embrace them, and attempt to blend this doctrine with those that do really oppose it. And it will appear, that *true religion*, including principles and practice, *the religion of the Bible*, and that only, is, in every part, consistent with God's punishing the wicked forever; so as to bear a friendly aspect to, and truly approve it. By this test, then, every doctrine and all hearts may be tried.

Here many particular doctrines, and different schemes of practical religion, might be brought into view, and examined by this test: But this will be omitted; and only one general character of all false religion mentioned, and tried by this rule: That is, *selfish religion*, as opposed to all disinterested, public affection. It is easy to see that selfishness cannot be reconciled to eternal punishment, on those grounds, and for the reasons, aside from which, or were it not for them, it would be undesirable, and not reasonable, viz. The glory of God and

and the greatest general good. As endless punishment is necessary to promote this, God approves of it, and has ordained it: But *in this view*, it is wholly opposed to selfishness: For that pays no regard to the honor of God, or the general good; but seeks only a private interest: And consequently, all selfish religion does oppose endless punishment. And it hence appears, that true religion consists in that benevolence, and that public, disinterested affection which is implied in it, which desires and seeks the glory of God, and the greatest public or general good; so as to subordinate *all* to this, and be reconciled to *that*, and acquiesce in it, be it what it will, which is best suited to answer this end; and opposes every thing, so far as it appears to be opposed to this: And that every degree of that selfishness, which is opposed to such benevolence, is opposed to God, and all his institutions and ways.

II. It may be hence inferred, that to believe and teach the salvation of all men is very dangerous and hurtful. This appears to be so, as it is contrary to the truth, so clearly revealed in the sacred oracles: Since every error, especially one so gross, and of such magnitude, must be dangerous, and of an evil tendency.

They whose religious exercises, whose love to God, &c. have their foundation in a belief, that there is no such thing as endless punishment, and that all mankind shall be happy forever; so that the belief of the contrary would put an end to all their love and religion, are certainly in a very dangerous way. All their religious affections, their love, hope and joy, will perish forever, when they are made to *know*, that the wicked shall go away into everlasting punishment: And they will be found enemies to the true God, and his wise administrations, and only fit to be cast into that everlasting fire. And all those, whose hope of future happineſs

piness is wholly founded on a belief and confidence, that none shall be miserable, are in a most dangerous situation. Their trust and confidence will perish: Their hope is as the spider's web, and shall be as the giving up of the ghost: This delusion now shuts their ears, and fortifies them against all warnings adapted to excite their fears, and awaken them to fly from the wrath to come; and has a direct & mighty tendency to sink them down into carelessness, and neglect of all religion; and to encourage them in worldly, and vicious gratifications and pursuits, while they flatter themselves, and say, "We shall have peace, though we walk in the imagination of our heart, and add drunkenness to thirst."

It is so evident, from reason and observation, that this is true of the doctrine, *That there is no punishment for the wicked in the future state*: That not only they who believe their punishment will be endless; but those who think it will be temporary, though it may be long and dreadful, without hesitation pronounce the former a licentious, dangerous doctrine; * while they who hold the latter, say this has no such bad tendency.

But, if this subject be properly considered, it will doubtless appear, that the latter has the same, and an equally bad, and dangerous tendency, with the former.

We find that when sinners are awakened to a sense of their danger and the evil case in which they are, so as to think in earnest of reformation and embracing the gospel, in order to salvation; it is always under some conviction and sense of *endless* misery, as the certain consequence of persisting in their evil ways. And if they can be made to believe there is no such punishment; but that they shall certainly be happy forever, whatever be

---

* It may be added, that, on this principle, all oaths, or solemn appeals to God for the truth of what men say, which
are

be their character and conduct in this world; this will remove their great attention and pressing concern; and give them ease, while they go on in their sins. And every person, who has been in any degree properly attentive to his eternal interest, and will consult his own feelings, must own, that it is unspeakably more dreadful and alarming, to think of being lost and miserable Forever, and view himself in the utmost danger of it, than to see himself in danger of only a temporary punishment. The awakened sinner, in fearful expectation

A a of

are so necessary in civil government, are perfectly useless: For he who sweareth falsely has no judge or future judgment to fear or regard; and will be as happy in the future state, as he who feareth a false oath. And no degree of unfaithfulness, deceit and unrighteousness, or indulgence of any lust whatever, will be the least disadvantage to a man, after he leaves the body. And no fear of any evil, after death, can take place, to be the least restraint from putting an end to his own life, or the life of others: But the confident expectation of happiness in the other world, becomes a strong inducement to put himself, and those nearly connected with him, out of this world: Especially, when worldly circumstances and prospects are dark and disagreeable; that he may free himself and them, from the evils of this life. Therefore, if it were possible that this doctrine should be really believed and spread, would it not sap the foundation of civil government; introduce the greatest evils in human society, by the prevalence of the unrestrained lusts of men; put an end to all mutual confidence of men in each other; and promote suicide and murders innumerable? According to this doctrine, the greatest enemy of God in the world has the staff in his own hands; and whenever the indulgence of his lusts has rendered this life disagreeable, he may defy the punishing hand of his Maker, and push himself into perfect and endless happiness, in a moment! This is observed, not as an argument, or *from the least desire*, that the civil power should be exerted to put a stop to this doctrine: But to demonstrate that tenet to be a gross delusion, which is pregnant with such fatal evils to human society.

of destruction, as the consequence of the way he has taken, will express the feelings of his mind, in the following language. "O! If the destruction which is like to be my portion were not *endless*, it would be tolerable and light, compared with being miserable *forever.* The thought of this drinks up my spirit, and draws over my soul a horrid gloom, and sinking despair; and fills it with anguish and torture, which nothing else could do. If I could be sure this punishment will ever come to an end, and I be forever happy, after all; this would be better than ten thousand worlds to me; and turn all my sorrow and distress into peace and joy." And let such a sinner be persuaded that this is true, and his concern, that laid him under great restraints before, will subside, and his strong aversion to holiness, and powerful, pressing inclination to indulge his darling lusts, and live in sin, will hold him fast in this course, with a great degree of security and ease. And he is never like to be alarmed again, or persuaded to alter his course, by all the terrors *they* can preach to him, who tell him, he is in no danger of endless misery, but, let him live as he will, he must be eternally happy. ‡

If the sinner be told, and is made to believe, that though he live and die in his evil courses, he will be punished

---

‡ It has been said, That a long future punishment, including very great and terrible sufferings, even till the sinner is brought to repentance, is sufficient effectually to restrain men from their wicked courses; yea, *more effectually,* than endless punishment; because the latter is *incredible,* and will not therefore affect the mind. But is not this said in opposition to the highest reason, and all experience? Whether endless punishment does "exceed all belief," let him judge who has perused the preceding inquiry. And it is easy to see, that the fear of a finite punishment must have unspeakably less influence on the sinner, than of an endless one, if it will have any at all, in this case.

punished in the future state, only till he is willing to repent; this will be no matter of terror to him, or have the least tendency to reform him; but the contrary, to an amazing degree: For he is disposed to think himself not very guilty and ill deserving; and that his lusts and vicious courses are in a great degree innocent and harmless; and therefore, that his punishment will not be very great. Besides, he has so good an opinion of himself, that he has not the least doubt, but he shall be willing to repent immediately, when the present objects of his lusts and pursuits shall be at an end, and he can have no more pleasure and happiness in the way of sin; and consequently, it is impossible to make him fear any length of punishment, on this plan, or even any at all; because he is confident he shall escape it all, by repentance and submission to God. Therefore, the threatning of *such* a punishment, will have no more influence on the sinner, to awaken and reform him, than none at all; while he is assured he shall have everlasting happiness, and shall suffer no longer than he shall continue obstinate and impenitent.

How many millions of sinners have there been, who have quieted their fears, and encouraged themselves to go on in vicious courses, by presuming, that in their last moments they would repent and cry for mercy, if they did not do it before; and that they should then find favor with God, when they could enjoy the pleasures of sin no longer? And if this presumption has given such encouragement to continue in sin, when they had no security that they should have opportunity to repent, or assurance that God would then regard them, if in their last moments they should cry to him for mercy: How much more encouragement to licentiousness is given to sinners, by assuring them from the word of God that they shall be eternally happy, be they as vicious

they

they will, in this life; and that they shall not suffer a minute longer than they continue impenitent; and shall have as good and better opportunity to repent and cry for mercy, in the other world, than they have here, as they will not have the same tempting objects and allurements to sin, nor can have any pleasure or advantage by it; and it can never be too late to repent?

This being the case, it is no wonder it is confirmed by fact and experience. Where is the person, who has been awakened and reformed from a course of sin, by being told, that if he did not repent and reform in this life; though he must after all be eternally happy; yet, he should be punished in the other world, till he was willing to repent and be happy? It is presumed no such person is to be found, nor can the argument be given up, till some instances to the contrary are produced: Especially, since there are so many instances, on the other side, to confirm it. Who are the persons that are most pleased with the doctrine of universal salvation, and forwardest to embrace it? The most sober, virtuous, benevolent people, or they who are at the greatest distance from all this? And what improvement is evidently made of it by multitudes? Is it not to flatter and confirm them in licentiousness? Is it not peculiarly suited to this corrupt age? And does it not promise to promote, as far as it shall spread, a torrent of libertinism, in the practice of all manner of vice and wickedness? Every serious, attentive person will easily decide these questions.

How can that doctrine be agreeable to the gospel, represented by Christ and the inspired writers, as not suited to please wicked men; but to excite their displeasure and hatred; which is so very agreeable to wicked men and infidels now; so that they will rather renounce the bible and turn Deists, than give it up? Yea, all open enemies to the sacred oracles, if they be-

lieve

lieve a future state, are friends to the doctrine of universal happiness.

Can that doctrine be agreeable to Christ, or displeasing to the devil, which is so pleasing to wicked men in this world, and has such manifest influence to flatter and confirm them in their evil courses?

III. In the light of eternal punishment, we have a most affecting sight of the awfully dangerous, and extremely miserable and wretched state of all those who are in their impenitence, going the broad way that leads to this destruction: And hence learn, what tender concern, and bowels of compassion ought to be exercised towards them; and the reasonableness of being ready and engaged to take all possible pains, and use all proper means, that they may be plucked as brands from everlasting burnings.

There are many instances of great temporary calamity and wretchedness, in this world, which render persons objects of most sensible compassion. Such instances of misery often moved the compassion of our benevolent Saviour, when he was on earth; and he wrought many miracles for their relief. But this misery is nothing to that now in view. All the evil that men ever did, or can suffer, in this world, bears no proportion to the evil case of one sinner, who is cast into hell; from whence he cannot be delivered, so long as God shall exist. This evil, indeed, is not yet actually come upon them; but they are in the utmost danger of it, and will soon have it fixed upon them forever, unless, by some means, they can be recovered from their present course. This case then, above all others, calls for the compassion of the benevolent; and is most suited to raise it to the greatest height, and animate to the most earnest and unwearied endeavours, to relieve and save them. The compassion of St. Paul was excited

cited, by seeing men in this case, which caused "great heaviness, and continual sorrow in his heart;" and engaged him to "warn every one night and day with tears," and made him willing to do and suffer any thing, "If *by any means* he might save some;" and led him even to wish himself accursed from Christ, if this might effect the salvation of his brethren the Jews.

It is owing to unbelief, and great stupidity and senselessness, respecting eternal punishment, that they who are exposed to it, so that nothing but the tender thread of life, liable to break every minute, holds them up from this destruction, can make themselves easy, and feel so secure; and do not lament and weep, and turn their laughter into mourning, and their joy into heaviness; and fall into the greatest distress and horror. And what but an awful degree of this same stupidity, can be the reason, that the benevolent friends of mankind are not more affected with the misery of the wicked; and so little moved with compassion, while they are daily surrounded by such infinitely miserable objects; and are so negligent of means, that might be used for their relief?

Who can fully express the unreasonableness and folly of exercising great concern and anxiety about temporal calamities; and taking much pains to prevent their coming on near relations and friends, or deliver them from those which are upon them; while there is not the least concern, nor any pains taken, to deliver them from infinitely greater evil, even eternal destruction.

Is there not a great degree of practical denial of the doctrine of eternal punishment, among professing christians; while they feel and express no more tender concern and compassion for sinners, who are in such eminent danger of this punishment, if it be a reality; and use no more means to reclaim and save them? How
ought

ought they to put on bowels of mercies and kindness towards them, and treat them with the greatest love, tenderness and compassion, patience and longsuffering, while they are taking the most likely methods for their help? If Christians were thoroughly attentive to this, and did express their compassion for sinners, in all proper ways, it would remove one argument many think they have, that there is no such punishment; viz. That Christians themselves do not appear really to believe it, while they profess to do it: And it would tend to make eternal misery more of a reallity to them, and to gain their attention, and affect their hearts.

How unbecoming the profession of Christians is it, to be unmoved and inactive in this case! Especially, to converse and conduct so as tends to prevent the salvation of others, and destroy them forever! Instead of being with Christ, and gathering with him; they are against him, and doing the work of the great destroyer of souls. And how guilty must the ministers of the gospel and parents be; what an unbecoming and monstrously cruel part do they act, when, instead of faithfulness and benevolence to the souls immediately under their care, they speak and conduct, in a manner which tends to their eternal ruin, and so become their destroyers! These not only imitate *the destroyer*; but their sin in destroying souls forever, is, in many respects, much more aggravated, than his.

IV. This subject will be closed with the following address:

First, To those who have been by some means led into a disbelief of the doctrine of endless punishment; and those who are in doubt about it; and do not yet determine, whether there will be any such punishment or not.

If any of either of these, have read the foregoing
sheets

sheets, and shall be disposed still to read on; they are desired seriously to consider, whether the doctrine of eternal punishment is not as clearly revealed, and as well supported by scripture and reason, as any truth whatsoever; and what dangerous presumption it is to reject it, until they can find a full and satisfactory answer to the scriptures and arguments, which have been adduced in favor of it. And such must be warned of the danger of rejecting this doctrine, through prejudice; and a fond inclination and desire, that the contrary doctrine should be true. In this view, they are intreated to consider the following things.

1. The scriptures represent the truth there revealed, as disagreeable to wicked men; and that, for this reason, they are disposed to dislike and reject it. Our Saviour says, "*Every one* that doth evil, hateth the light, neither cometh to the light, lest his deeds should be reproved." And such are represented as "saying to the seers, *See not*; and to the prophets, Prophesy not unto us right things, speak unto us SMOOTH THINGS, prophesy deceits, cause the holy one of Israel to cease from before us." The Divine character is disagreeable to them. Therefore, when the prophets prophesied falsely, the degenerate people *loved to have it so*, and greedily embraced the delusion.

You who are conscious you are yet in your sins; that your hearts and practice are not conformable to the dictates of reason and word of God, ought not to conclude any doctrine to be wrong, because it is not agreeable to your way of thinking, and is displeasing to your inclinations and hearts. You must be cautioned, and warned of your danger, in the case before us. What if you should, through the sinful prejudice and evil bias of your minds, form your hopes of eternal happiness upon the fond conceit that none will be miserable

rable forever; and when it shall be too late, find yourselves mistaken, and be plunged into that very endless misery, which you was persuaded had no existence; and perhaps even ridiculed those who asserted it! Take heed lest this awful disappointment, this infinite evil, come upon you!

2. The first lie that was told in this world, was in the words of Satan, the father of lies, to our mother Eve: "YE SHALL NOT SURELY DIE," in order to induce her to rebel against God, and ruin herself. And he has been propagating this lie and deception, among mankind, ever since; by which men have flattered themselves, that they should have peace, though they walked after the evil inclinations of their own hearts; and it has proved the ruin of multitudes. And have you not reason to fear; yea, may you not be certain, when it is asserted, that no man shall perish forever, for any sin he can commit in this life, though he obstinately persist in it till death; but, notwithstanding all possible rebellion, shall be happy forever; this is the same lie, revived and propagated by Satan, and those unhappy persons, who are taken in his snare? It certainly looks just like it: And are you willing to be taken in such a snare, and perish forever?

3. The sacred oracles represent wicked men as inclined to flatter themselves, that evil will not come upon them, when they are upon the brink of destruction. Psal. x. 6. "The wicked hath said in his heart, I shall not be removed; for I shall never be in adversity." Isai. xxviii. 5. "Because ye have said, We have made a covenant with death, and with hell are we at agreement; when the overflowing scourge shall pass through, it shall not come unto us." Deu. xxix. 18, 19. "Lest there should be among you a root that beareth gall and wormwood; and it come to pass *when he heareth the words of this curse, that he bless himself in his heart, saying, I shall have peace, though I walk in the imagination of mine heart to add drunkenness to thirst.*" 1 Thess. v. 3. "For when they shall say, *Peace and safety*; then sudden destruction cometh upon them, and they shall not escape." This is the natural attendant of sin, thus to blind and delude the sinner; and lead him to flatter himself, that he shall escape the evil which is hastening upon him. And if you begin to lose the fears of future punishment, which perhaps you once had, and to think, and grow confident, that you shall have peace and eternal

ternal life, tho' you walk after the imagination of your own heart, and indulge every lust, have you not reason to think you are an instance of this very self-flattery and delusion, described in the scriptures now cited? If this be not the very thing, what can it be? Awake, and tremble, O sinner, for verily, *Thou art the man!*

4 The character of *false prophets*, in the scripture, is, that they flatter men in their sins, and prophesy smooth things, promising peace and safety to men, when destruction is coming upon them: And, on the contrary, the true prophets declared there was no peace to the wicked, and denounced evil and certain destruction which was coming upon them, unless they repented: And this recommended the former to the multitude, who caressed and spoke well of them; and at the same time rendered the latter disagreeable, and brought upon them hatred and ill treatment.

This observation might be illustrated by referring to a great number of particular passages of scripture.——————The attentive reader of the bible must be sensible of this. Only the following will be recited now. Jer. xxiii. 16, 17. " Thus saith the Lord of hosts, Hearken not unto the words of the prophets that prophesy unto you; they make you vain. They say still unto them that despise me, The Lord hath said, *Ye shall have peace*: And they say unto *every one* that walketh after the imagination of his own heart, *No evil shall come upon you.*" Ezek. xiii. 10. Of false prophets it is said, " They have seduced my people, saying, *Peace*, and there was no peace." Ver. 22. " With lies ye have strengthened the hands of the wicked, that he should not turn from his wicked way, *by promising him* LIFE."

Let those who are now addressed, seriously consider, whether they who promise eternal happiness to you, whatever be your character in this world; so that you cannot miss of it by any course of sin whatever, do not take upon them the very character which the bible gives of false prophets: And whether they, who, on the contrary, hold forth endless destruction, as the certain portion of the impenitent sinner; and those other doctrines which are connected with this, and are so disagreeable to wicked men in general, do not appear in the character of true prophets and teachers. And whether, by embracing the former, and rejecting and hating the latter, you will not act just as those deluded, wicked men did, who were pleased with the prophets who preached peace to them, and hated and persecuted those of the contrary character.

Be entreated to think of this, as you value your own souls, and would not be flattered to your *eternal* ruin. Think of it, with an unprejudiced, honest mind, until you are able to give a rational, satisfactory answer: And is it possible it should be in the negative?

5. When all the evidence from scripture, supported by reason, which has been produced; together with the preceding observations, are honestly considered and weighed; is it possible that any one should be able to stand forth and say, "I am *absolutely certain*, that all mankind will be eternally happy; and that he stands on a safe and sure foundation, who has no other ground but this, to build his assurance of everlasting life upon?" If you cannot do this, as you certainly cannot, unless your delusion be remarkably strong; but must own you are far from being absolutely certain, that all shall be happy; then why will you adhere to this, and trust in such an uncertainty for salvation, however probable you may think the doctrine to be; and neglect the only way in which you may be *absolutely certain*, and build on the most sure ground?

God hath laid in Zion *a sure foundation*, a tried, precious corner stone; and whosoever believeth on him, shall not be ashamed of his hope, shall never be destroyed. Here is the most perfect security, established by innumerable express promises, made by him who cannot lie: He who believeth on Christ, with that faith which implies love and obedience to him, shall not perish, but have everlasting life. How unreasonably do you act; of what folly and rashness are you guilty, if you neglect and refuse this great and sure salvation, which is offered to you; and you may be absolutely sure you shall have everlasting life, if you will accept of it; and trust to that which, at most, is no more than probable, and may fail you, after all! This is neglecting a certainty, for the sake of an uncertainty, at best, in an affair of the highest moment. Such conduct would be thought madness in any temporal, worldly matter; why then will you be guilty of it, when your whole, your eternal interest is depending? Indeed there is no probability that such folly and infatuation will end well; but a certainty, that if you take this course, and neglect Christ and the great salvation now, you cannot escape everlasting destruction, from the presence of the Lord and the glory of his power. "*Now* consider this, ye that forget God, left he tear you in pieces, and there be none to deliver."

SECONDLY, This address turns to those who profess to believe the doctrine of endless punishment; and know they are not Christians; who own themselves to be constantly exposed to everlasting destruction; and that this must be their portion, if they should die while in their present state: And yet, are in a great measure secure and easy, while they are neglecting the great salvation; and many of them go on in open and unrestrained wickedness.

Dear, infatuated souls, how can you be insensible, if you will think seriously a minute, that you are in a most dangerous wretched case, which calls for the pity of all the benevolent, and their earnest prayers, and friendly endeavours for your relief? And though all of this kind, has hitherto had no apparent success, yet the attempt must be repeated; and you are to be reproved, rebuked and exhorted, with all tenderness, longsuffering and doctrine, or instruction, it peradventure God will give you repentance; and you may recover yourselves out of the snare of the devil, who are taken captive by him at his will. Think not them your enemies who tell you the truth, whatever disagreeable and painful feelings it may give you.

Be entreated, as you love your own souls, not to hearken to the infinuations of those, who would persuade you there is no such dreadful evil as endless punishment to fear. There are such, and many are greedily swallowing the bait, and caught fast in the fatal snare; from which it is much to be feared they will never be recovered. You are not out of danger. Take heed to yourselves, left you should be induced to believe this fatal lie, by those who, with all their cunning craftiness, lie in wait to deceive. For while they promise you peace, liberty and eternal life,——they themselves must perish forever in their own delusion, unless they repent and believe on Christ, before they leave this world.

Attend to the evidence there is, from the holy scriptures,

of

of the certainty of endless punishment; and think of it, till your minds are established in the truth, and it becomes a reality to you. Be persuaded to meditate much upon the dreadfulness of this punishment. You may be sure you cannot imagine it to be greater than it will be, or conceive of the thousandth part of the dreadfulness of it. Think often, yea, constantly, how dreadful it will be to find yourselves *lost forever*; plunged into perfect, inexpressible misery, in absolute despair of deliverance, or the least mitigation of punishment to all eternity! Never, never, to have another agreeable thought or sensation, in the midst of the most disagreeable, horrid company; suffering the most keen distress and torture, which will be poured in upon you from every quarter, while you know you have not a friend in the universe to help or pity you; under the awful and most sensible frowns and curse of the infinitely terrible Jehovah, who will live forever and ever to punish you; your thoughts swiftly, and irrisistibly running forward, and fixing on *eternal, endless duration*; and the more you dwell on this, the higher will your misery and anguish arise: At the same time, with the keenest remorse, reflecting that you have brought yourselves to this infinitely dreadful end, by your own amazing folly, by constantly, through your whole life, rejecting the offers of pardon and salvation, kindly made to you, and urged upon you, by the infinitely benevolent Saviour. Think of all this, and much more, which, by seriously attending to the representation given in scripture of future punishment, will naturally be suggested to your mind.

Don't forget a moment, in what an infinitely dangerous situation you are: On the brink of the bottomless pit, where are everlasting burnings; having nothing to secure you from sinking down to hell, being held out of it, only by the hand of him whose goodness you are abusing, and whom you are constantly provoking, in a manner dreadful to think of, tho' it can't be fully conceived, to let you sink forever: And by this be warned to fly from the wrath to come.

And remember, that the Lord Jesus Christ, the mighty glorious Redeemer, now invites you to look unto him, that you may be saved from this infinitely dreadful, everlasting destruction, and you are called and commanded to repent and come unto him, that you may have eternal life: And it must

therefore

therefore be altogether your own inexcusable fault, if you perish by refusing to obey his call: And your rejecting him, and *thus going to hell*, will necessarily render your punishment inexpressibly greater and more dreadful, than it would be, if there had been no Saviour, and you never had such an offer. Why then will you not *now* believe on the Lord Jesus Christ, and be saved?

How shocking is the sight of all openly vicious persons! The unrighteous and oppressor——The evil speaker and contentious——The adulterer, fornicator, and all lewd, obscene persons. The drunkard, and all liars. These shall not inherit the kingdom of God; but must have their part in the lake which burneth with fire and brimstone, unless they repent.

And what will become of all these who refuse to pay any regard to God, to religion, and divine institutions! Who wholly neglect the bible, disregard the sabbath, and all the ordinances of Christ; who restrain prayer, and will not call upon God? The Lord will come in a day when they look not for him, and at an hour when they think not, and will cut them asunder, and appoint them their portion with *unbelievers*, where shall be endless weeping, wailing and gnashing of teeth.

There are multitudes among us, and the number is increasing, who not only take the sacred name of their Maker in vain; but trifle and sport with that which is above all things dreadful, *eternal damnation*. They will not only wish damnation to others, but damn their own souls and bodies, or call upon God to damn them, many hundreds of times in a day. It is not probable any of these will read this; but it is earnestly to be desired, that by some means, the reality and amazing dreadfulness of damnation might so impress their minds, as effectually to prevent their ever uttering another profane curse; and they be made sensible of their astonishing stupidity, impiety and wickedness, in thus cursing themselves and others; by which they treasure up wrath against the day of wrath; and by every such curse add to their eternal misery, when their cursing will become a reality, and *pour into their own bowels like water, and into their bones like oil*, if their repentance do not prevent.

There are others, who for the sake of some sensual, momentary gratification, or the vain amusements and follies of

this

this life, are giving up their eternal happiness, and plunging themselves into endless destruction. O, that they would attend and hearken to the kind warning and advice given to them by Christ! "If thy hand or foot offend thee, cut them off; or if thine eye offend thee (i. e. cause thee to offend or fail) pluck it out, and cast it from thee: It is better for thee to enter into life halt or maimed, or with one eye, than having two hands or two feet, or two eyes, to be cast into hell, into the fire that never shall be quenched; where their worm dieth not, and the fire is not quenched."

How many *worldly minded persons* are there, who for the sake of the pursuit, or the possession and enjoyments of this world, are every day selling their souls, and giving them up to be tormented forever. Let such consider what they are doing, or what inexpressible folly and madness they are guilty; by realizing what it is to be *lost*, to go away into everlasting punishment; and let them attend to the awakening words of Christ, "What is a man profited, if he shall gain the whole world and lose his own soul? Or what shall a man give in exchange for his soul?"

Others there are, who having been restrained from the gross open vices which they see practised by many, and being insensible of the vile nature and ill desert of *all* sin, and ignorant of the wickedness of their own hearts; think they don't deserve to be punished forever, and therefore are confident they are in no danger of this dreadful evil. And others depend on their prayers and supposed good works; thinking them so deserving, as to be sufficient to secure them from future punishment. All these would be sensible of their mistake and delusion, did they understand and believe what is said of Christ, "Neither is there salvation in any other: For there is no other name under heaven given among men, whereby we must be saved," Or did they attend to the divine law, and let that come to their consciences and hearts, in its true meaning and strictness, *cursing* every one who continueth not in all things written and required therein; for by this their sins which are now hid from them, would revive, and all their vain hopes forever die.

In sum, whatever be the different circumstances and conduct of men, in this life, if they be no *real Christians*, they are in danger of eternal fire; and if they are in their present state

Sect. VI.

state and character, will be punished with everlasting destruction from the presence of the Lord, and the glory of his power. For the Redeemer himself hath said, and it cannot be reversed, but will be verified in all, "He that believeth [the gospel] and is baptised, shall be saved; BUT HE THAT BELIEVETH NOT, SHALL BE DAMNED. AMEN.

" He that has ears to hear, let him hear."

F I N I S.

The Reader is desired to correct the following Errors of the Press.
Page 58, line 18, read *renders*.
P. 74, l. 7, from the bottom, read *not*.
P. 75, in the Note, l. 9. read *comes*.
P. 77, l. 5, from bot. for *in* read *on*.
P. 85, l. 2, fr. b. read *spirits of devils*.
P. 104, l. 21, the comma after *imply*, should be after *it*.
P. 109, l. 4, fr. b. read *sufficient*.
P. 117, l. 15, for *any* read *an*.
P. 138, l. 11, from bot. read *should be*.
P. 155, l. 20, read *becomes*.

www.ingramcontent.com/pod-product-compliance
Lightning Source LLC
Chambersburg PA
CBHW032224230426
43666CB00033B/1440